FUTURING BLACK LIVES

Independent Black Institutions and the Literary Imagination

Maisha T. Winn

VANDERBILT UNIVERSITY PRESS
Nashville, Tennesee

Copyright 2025 Vanderbilt University Press
All rights reserved
First printing 2025

Library of Congress Cataloging-in-Publication Data

Names: Winn, Maisha T. author
Title: Futuring Black lives : independent Black institutions and the
  literary imagination / Maisha T. Winn.
Description: Nashville, Tennessee : Vanderbilt University Press, 2025. |
  Series: Black lives and liberation | Includes bibliographical references
  and index.
Identifiers: LCCN 2025004985 (print) | LCCN 2025004986 (ebook) | ISBN
  9780826507921 hardcover | ISBN 9780826507914 paperback | ISBN
  9780826507938 epub | ISBN 9780826507945 pdf
Subjects: LCSH: African American children--Education | African American
  children--Books and reading | Institute of Positive Education (Chicago,
  Ill.)--History | Black Arts movement | Discrimination in
  education--United States | Mentoring in education--United States |
  Academic achievement--Social aspects--United States
Classification: LCC LC2771 .W56 2025 (print) | LCC LC2771 (ebook) | DDC
  371.829/96073--dc23/eng/20250402
LC record available at https://lccn.loc.gov/2025004985
LC ebook record available at https://lccn.loc.gov/2025004986

Front cover image: Yaoundé Olu cover for *Black Books Bulletin*'s Summer 1976 issue, "Black
People and the Future." Reprinted with permission from Third World Press Foundation.

Futuring Black Lives

BLACK LIVES & LIBERATION

SERIES EDITORS
Brandon Byrd, *Vanderbilt University*
Zandria F. Robinson, *Rhodes College*
Christopher Cameron, *University of North Carolina, Charlotte*

BLACK LIVES MATTER. What began as a Twitter hashtag after the 2013 acquittal of George Zimmerman for the murder of Trayvon Martin has since become a widely recognized rallying cry for black being and resistance. The series aims are two-fold: 1) to explore social justice and activism by black individuals and communities throughout history to the present, including the Black Lives Matter movement and the evolving ways it is being articulated and practiced across the African Diaspora; and 2) to examine everyday life and culture, rectifying well-worn "histories" that have excluded or denied the contributions of black individuals and communities or recast them as entirely white endeavors. Projects draw from a range of disciplines in the humanities and social sciences and will first and foremost be informed by "peopled" analyses, focusing on everyday actors and community folks.

In the Shadow of Powers: Dantes Bellegarde in Haitian Social Thought,
by Patrick Bellegarde-Smith

Race, Religion, and Black Lives Matter: Essays on a Moment and a Movement,
edited by Christopher Cameron and Phillip L. Sinitiere

*Continually Working: Black Women, Community Intellectualism,
and Economic Justice in Postwar Milwaukee,* by Crystal M. Moten

From Rights to Lives: The Evolution of the Black Freedom Struggle, edited
by Charles W. McKinney and Françoise N. Hamlin

Black Gurl Reliable: Pedagogies of Vulnerability and Transgression,
by Dominique C. Hill

Haiti and the Revolution Unseen: The Persistence of the Decolonial Imagination,
by Natalie M. Léger

For Obasi and Zafir

Contents

Foreword by Robin D. G. Kelley   *ix*

INTRODUCTION. When Histories and Futures Meet   1

1. "What About Our Tomorrows?": Institution Building
for Black Lives   21

2. "We Are Studying to Advance the Struggle": IPE Visionaries
Forecasting for Black Lives   39

3. Between "Precariousness" and "Possibility": The Emergence
of *Black Books Bulletin*   63

4. "There Is No Magic . . . Except the Magic of Truth":
Nation Building with Books for the Young   87

5. "The Present Passes . . . the Next Day—Mars": Futuring
for Black Lives   111

EPILOGUE. "We Are Not Revolutionaries. We Are Farmers."   121

Acknowledgments   125
Notes   129
Bibliography   147
Index   155

Foreword

Robin D.G. Kelley

"Goodbye Black Sambo," an article celebrating a new generation of Black children's literature, appeared in the November 1972 issue of *Ebony* magazine. Its author Carole A. Parks, a noted figure in the Chicago's Black Arts circle, credited Virginia Hamilton, John Steptoe, June Jordan, Ellen Tarry, Sharon Bell Mathis, and others for creating positive images of Black people in contrast to the racist representations common in "classic" children's literature.[1] The most striking feature of the article, for me at least, focuses not on the writers but a new generation of Black readers. Young patrons of the George Cleveland Hall branch of the Chicago Public Library, which served the predominantly Black South Side, were known to have "mutilated" books depicting Black people as "sambos" and "pickaninnies." "It insulted our Negro children," explained librarian Charlemae Hill Rollins. "They didn't want to be depicted that way. We knew that because they said so on the books. They would tear the pages out, take crayons and draw over them or write obscene things across them. They didn't do that to other books."[2]

Charlemae Rollins knew what she was talking about. Born in Mississippi to a family of Black educators, Rollins spent nearly three decades as the children's librarian for the G. C. Hall branch. As happened with Harlem's Schomburg Library, the branch became a beehive of cultural activity. Rollins and head librarian Vivian Harsh organized storytelling sessions, book clubs, Black history clubs, art exhibits, and readings by notables such as Richard Wright, Zora Neale Hurston, Langston Hughes,

Margaret Burroughs, Arna Bontemps, and Gwendolyn Brooks. While taking graduate classes at the University of Chicago, Rollins researched representations of race in children's literature and, at the request of the National Council of Teachers of English, published *We Build Together: A Reader's Guide to Negro Life and Literature for Elementary and High School Use* (1941). This influential pamphlet not only identified racist tropes in children's literature but provided a list of books with authentic Black characters and positive representations of Black life. After retiring in 1963, Rollins published several acclaimed books for young readers on African American political leaders, entertainers, and poets, including a biography of her friend Langston Hughes.[3]

Defacing books is the sort of thing that gets you barred from libraries or suspended from school, especially if you're Black. The whole premise of zero tolerance or "broken windows" policing is that disregard for, or destruction of, property is a gateway to more serious crimes. By this twisted logic, vandalizing precious library resources is not only evidence of a culture of criminality but of ignorance, anti-intellectualism, and ingratitude. It justifies library closures and defunding Black and Brown communities. But Charlemae Rollins and Carole Parks recognized what Maisha T. Winn establishes in this magnificent book: these kids were not vandals or criminals-in-training but victims of a kind of literary lynching. They were attempting to erase a past conjured up in the white imagination, to chart a different future. In other words, they were budding "futurists," seedlings cultivated by a generation of activists, artists, and educators who believed literacy and literature were essential tools in the struggle for Black liberation.

For Winn, "futuring" is a verb, a conscious, collective movement that involves critical education, creative cultural production, radical imagination, and independent Black institutions dedicated to self-determination and nation building. It is a world she knows intimately, from the Black community school established by her parents in the 1970s, Shule Jumamose, in Sacramento, to her research on Black-owned bookstores and cafes as crucial spaces of literacy and literary knowledge. *Futuring Black Lives* looks specifically at Chicago's Institute of Positive Education, founded by Haki R. Madhubuti and Dr. Carol D. Lee, and *Black Books Bulletin*, a formidable journal edited by Madhubuti for more than two decades. By linking the Black Arts Movement to the rise of Black independent education, Winn expands our understanding of the Black Arts Movement as a political and pedagogical project.

This is also a Chicago story. The Windy City is arguably the mecca for Black futuring. It is where pianist/composer Sun Ra established his Arkestra and found in the history and philosophy of ancient Egypt a path to a liberated future, or what he called "Alter-destiny." Chicago is also home to the Association for the Advancement of Creative Musicians, which established its own school in 1967 on the South Side less than two miles from the Institute of Positive Education. Indeed, they shared similar values and objectives. As trumpeter John Shenoy Jackson declared, "our basic thing is to protect our race, protect our Black children, protect our Black boys and girls and to raise them up to be strong and broad-shouldered and proud. This is the undercurrent . . . this is why we have the school, this is why we go and play free in schools sometimes, go out into the community."[4]

The point of creating community-based cultural institutions and launching journals such as *Black Books Bulletin* was not merely to build self-esteem, redeem Africa's past, or prove that Black people were human. Black humanity was never in question. The real question was how to survive the daily subjugation and violence of white *inhumanity*. During the 1960s and '70s, Black nationalists spoke earnestly about survival under what many characterized as a fascist regime perpetuating genocide (an indictment that, unfortunately, often included birth control and abortion). Given the frequent deployment of the National Guard to suppress urban rebellions and occupy American ghettoes, conspiratorial talk of secret concentration camps and chemical warfare were not far-fetched. After all, Black men were disappearing in prisons and dying at the hands of police or on the killing fields of Vietnam, heroin flooded Black neighborhoods, lead poisoning sickened poor Black children, and good paying industrial jobs simply disappeared.[5]

Futuring Black Lives shows that cultural literacy is as essential to survival as food, shelter, safety, and community. Education grounds a people in a shared past, a critical philosophy of struggle, and a vision of the future—what Haki Madhubuti calls the three pillars of Black education: Identity, Purpose, and Direction. If the image of Black kids discretely destroying racist library books represents a struggle for identity, the creation of the Institute of Positive Education and its uniquely democratic, liberatory, child-focused pedagogy embodies purpose and direction. In the face of an ongoing yet escalating war on education, on Black studies, on Black people, the history Winn recovers is as relevant now as it was in 1969. She found in the Black Arts Movement, and in the Institute of Positive Education in particular, alternative models for educating our children; for creating, circulating, and debating knowledge, art, and culture; and for imagining a world beyond our current reality. And therein lies perhaps the most important lesson of all: the future is not something we "wait" for; it is made in struggle, by movements forging new horizons—even in the face of fascism.

INTRODUCTION

When Histories
and Futures Meet

In the Winter 1974 issue of *Black Books Bulletin* literary journal, a black
and white image on the inside back cover shows fourteen African American
adults gathered around a long rectangular table; two other adults
are also engaged with the group, one atop a stool, slightly more elevated, and one standing (see Figure I.1). The barely visible communal
table—buried under papers, writing utensils, and even a baby's bottle—
appears to be a site of planning, decision making, thinking, and building. The presence of small children on several adults' laps signals that
caregiving was woven into that process. Flanked by full bookshelves, a
filing cabinet, and a portable chalkboard, the smiling man at the head of
the table has one of the children on his lap.[1] I recognized three adults.
The smiling man at the head of the table was Haki Madhubuti (formerly Don L. Lee), poet, essayist, professor of literature, and founder
of Third World Press, an independent Black publishing house in Chicago established in 1967. Seated on the elevated stool was Carol D. Lee
(née Carol Easton), former Chicago City College instructor, and later
award-winning learning scientist and professor emerita of Northwestern University. Jabari Mahiri (formerly Cleve Washington), a former
Chicago Public School teacher and later a professor of education, was
seated to the right of Madhubuti.

Madhubuti, Lee, and Mahiri, as well as other Black educators, artists,
parents, and everyday people, were part of the creation of the Institute

FIGURE I.1. Photo of the Institute of Positive Education (IPE) Baraza ya Kazi, published in their literary journal, *Black Books Bulletin*, Winter 1974 issue. Photographer: K. Kofi Moyo. Reprinted with permission.

of Positive Education (IPE, pronounced "ee-pay"), an Independent Black Institution (IBI) established in 1969 in Chicago, two years after Madhubuti established Third World Press.[2] IPE created and was responsible for an African-centered preschool, the New Concept Development Center; the Ujamaa Food Co-op; nutrition seminars; a small farm in Michigan; a summer camp; the Wachunga (youth) program; Nation Studies classes; a library; a book mobile; and a range of educational aids and publications, including the Black Pages pamphlet series and the *Black Books Bulletin* (the *Bulletin*) literary journal, which was published quarterly from 1971 to 1981. Madhubuti was the principal architect of these endeavors, Lee shaped the vision for the schools and education projects, and Mahiri served as the *Bulletin*'s managing editor for most of the journal's tenure.

IPE emerged during and was part of "the rise of IBIs," Black-owned and -operated institutions often housing schools, food cooperatives, and publications that were being established throughout the United States during the Black Arts Movement.[3] Typically situated between 1965 and 1975, the Black Arts Movement was the cultural arm of the Black Power Movement, and the visionaries in the photo—known collectively as IPE's Baraza ya Kazi (work council)—like IBI staff and leaders throughout the United States, worked to "educate and socialize" Black children to "assume their future roles" and also to provide Black families with tools to become "self-reliant" and "self-defining."[4] IPE's aim was to generate "self-reliance through self-work" and stakeholders worked collectively toward the "re-definition and re-education of [Black] people."[5] Notably, every child in the image of IPE's Baraza ya Kazi was on the lap of an adult who was not their parent, which was consistent with IPE's value of centering Black children and their belief that all adults were responsible for those children's well-being. Soyini Walton, IPE co-founder, science curriculum lead for their schools, and former principal for one of their charter schools, explained the proliferation of Black institutions in Chicago as she reflected on the photo of IPE visionaries:

> Possibilities. That is what this picture symbolizes to me. There is so much potential with what we're doing. This is like a breath of fresh air coming out of the Civil Rights Movement—and that was such drudgery. The Civil Right Movement was such a hard fight that involved a loss of life and all of that. Our attitude was, "Okay, let's put our stake in the stream right there." All those things have passed but we've got a new look on what the power of us can create as a group. The power of us. We're going to be positive. Thus the name, The Institute of Positive Education. There is so much potential and possibility. And we have a template on how we can get this thing done with very little resources, but we have each other.[6]

Futuring Black Lives: Independent Black Institutions and the Literary Imagination examines the work of Black institution builders during the Black Power and Black Arts Movements. What can we learn from Black institution builders that can support current efforts to design for equity, educate Black children, and engage in future-oriented pedagogy? How did IBIs, and IPE in particular, use Black print culture and publications such as the *Bulletin* as tools to imagine, forecast, and plan for Black lives? Published quarterly between 1971 and 1981, the *Bulletin* engaged readers' literary imaginations to promote Pan-Africanism, contextualize Black Cultural Nationalism, and promote Identity, Purpose, and Direction—the tenets of Black education and steps toward sustainable and thriving Black futures.

Futuring Black Lives examines how IBIs in the era of the Black Arts Movement, 1965 to 1975, used publications and print culture to leverage the power of the literary imagination in service of worldbuilding.[7] I focus on IPE and its visionaries as a case study. How did Black institution builders like the IPE visionaries position themselves as futurists? Why and how did they generate maps of and for the future that remain as print material archives? From what traditions and lived experiences did IPE visionaries emerge? What strategies and approaches did these Black institution builders collectively envision? How did they enact their vision in thoroughly integrated ways for Black children?

The black and white photo on the inside back cover of the Winter 1974 issue of the *Bulletin* became my compass in 2020. My husband and I were partners in transitioning our home into a school for our sons, first and third graders during and following initial COVID-19 "shelter-in-place" orders in California. Our own dining room table was covered with pamphlets, newspapers, journals, and other ephemera created by independent Black institutions during the late 1960s and throughout the 1970s. I was arm's length from the site of one of my son's new classrooms, and I felt kinship with the men and women in the photo and their work to build forward by/while centering children's needs in a life season of rapid change, so many unknowns regarding what the future would bring.

The early months of the pandemic brought a pause to my analysis of historical documents from as early as 1964 as I turned to collect signals about the future of education. Institute for the Future defines a *signal* as a "small or local innovation or disruption that has potential to grow in scale and geographic distribution."[8] Some of the signals I collected included stories of families finding ways to reclaim their children's education by creating cooperatives and by homeschooling—when schools initially closed, and even after classes eventually resumed online and became accessible.[9] After more than one billion people worldwide witnessed the murder of George Floyd by a police officer in Minneapolis, Minnesota, in May 2020, Black families increasingly expressed reluctance to send their children back to school. This was not about COVID-19, per se, but parents' consideration of (and fear for) their children's social and emotional well-being, given the pervasive oppression, weight, and violence—physical, emotional, ideological, and symbolic—of anti-Blackness and state-sanctioned violence against Black people.[10] I felt the same kinship with these parents as with those from the generation before ours who established IBIs: we all sought to (re)claim our children's education against the backdrop of harmful, racialized patterns and experiences in the US.

From Sacramento to Chicago, and Back: Who Am I and Why Am I Here?

I feign no neutrality in this work. A daughter of Black institution builders who were inspired by the Black Arts and Black Power Movements, I consider myself a beneficiary of these early efforts to disrupt Black self-hatred and promote the three pillars of Black education: Identity, Purpose, and Direction.[11] This "way of living" inspired my parents to engineer my childhood with purposeful reframings of Blackness as an asset in a world steeped in anti-Black messaging. They drew from the well of creativity unfolding in Black institutions across the country: IPE in Chicago, The East in Brooklyn, the African Free School in Newark, and many others. I was born in 1972. The following year, Haki Madhubuti published his foundational text, *From Plan to Planet Life Studies: The Need for Afrikan Minds and Institutions*, which sought to move theory and ideology into practice and action through a series of theoretical and conceptual essays on Black education, art, and politics, anchored with a "functional reading list" in the closing pages. Elsewhere, I have described my life as an embodiment of Haki Madhubuti's *plan* and myself as inhabitant of his *planet*.[12] I am an ethnographer by training and a historian by necessity. *Futuring Black Lives* examines primary source materials from a family archive, currently in my possession, I refer to as the Shule Jumamose Archive, curated by my father as he and my mother shaped and refined a vision for that school.

My parents met during an era of institution building, and their shared commitments to Black freedom and futures defined their work in the community and at home. Inspired by a conference in Sacramento entitled "Gettin' it Together: A Service Conference on Black Survival" in 1971 (see Figure I.2), my late mother, Cheryl Ann Fisher (then Cheryl

FIGURE I.2. Poster advertising Sacramento State College's "Gettin' It Together!" conference in May 1971. Source: Shule Jumamose Archive

Ann Smith), with Bertha Gorman and Martha Reid, two other concerned Black women who were students at California State University in Sacramento, organized to create an IBI they called Shule Jumamose (Saturday School).[13] Shule Jumamose's founders and the visionaries who supported them wanted to provide Black children with opportunities for positive identity development through classes in numerous disciplines coupled with immersive experiences like Sacramento's first public Kwanzaa event and an African American film festival with the students' families and the larger community.[14]

My mother recruited my father as her partner in life and in Shule Jumamose and tasked him with developing Shule Jumamose's curriculum and curating experiences for students and their families. Prior to joining the Shule Jumamose movement, my father was completing his dissertation and teaching classes at Sacramento City College (SCC), where he was among the faculty who helped create the Oak Park School of Afro-American Thought, which provided opportunities for residents of Sacramento's Oak Park neighborhood to take SCC classes, for credit. SCC set up trailers as classrooms, and my father and other instructors taught a range of courses, including Ghetto economics, Black drama, social science, and history. Despite his positive experiences and affiliation with SCC, my father understood the importance and opportunity of transitioning to an independent Black educational institutional context (see Figure I.3):

> Those of us connected to the [Oak Park] School of Afro-American Thought knew that Sacramento City College ultimately would have the final say and mutual control over the activities . . . some of us broke away to form Shule Jumamose—an independent school. We [wanted to] make our own rules . . . following the ideas and good vibes of the Black Arts Movement, which was more than arts. . . . It was a way of living and it was life itself for some people. The [Black Arts Movement] formed a perfect blanket for us to wrap ourselves in and enjoy the moment. And the moment was the thinking that Black people should have [our] own institutions . . . be able to make [our] own decisions for [our]selves and future generations . . . that kind of self-reliance and self-determination as represented by the seven principles were the things we lived by or wanted to live by and [were] challenged to live by.[15]

As they imagined the operational dynamics and future of Shule Jumamose, my parents looked to IBIs across the country, subscribing to periodicals, sending donations, and requesting curricular guides from the IPE in Chicago, The East in Brooklyn, the African Free School in Newark, and others. In addition to curricular guides, journals, newspapers, newspaper clippings, Black Studies curricula, and other IBI ephemera, the Shule Jumamose Archive captures that school's own brief (1971–1974), yet compelling, journey through newspaper articles; photographs of the school, students, and teachers; lesson plans; curricular guides;

and expectations for teachers. This compiled archival material could be viewed as a "how to" guide for building an IBI—but it is more expansive than that lens allows. Offering roadmaps for and to the future, these materials introduce a way of being, knowing, and engaging that shaped the culture of one small IBI in Northern California, and they connect those efforts to a larger vision of/for Black education nationwide. It is important to consider that these archival contents were collected by everyday people, my parents, in active pursuit of ideas and information about how to (re)imagine the purpose of education for Americans of African descent. These resources were then carefully preserved, indicating their perceived usefulness in and for other times and places. For example, when I encountered a large red piece of posterboard with a short statement entitled "All Learning," in handwriting I recognized as my mother's, in the Shule Jumamose Archive, I decided to display it for my children and myself in our pandemic homeschool:

All learning is not fun . . .
Some learning is tedious,
Some learning is repetitious.
But we cannot be Black and Proud and Dumb,
Therefore, we must learn
For we are the New Black Nation.[16]

I continued to explore the Shule Jumamose Archive with even more gratitude for the historical signals they contained. Whereas innovation is frequently situated as an entirely new concept, idea, or something in the future, historical signals reposition innovation as having historical roots and foundations. IPE's quarterly journal, the *Bulletin*, one of several complete sets of publications, stood out to me because of its ambitious aims to imagine and speak to literate and literary interlocuters who viewed reading and writing as part and parcel of freedom struggles in the tradition of Black Americans—both enslaved and free. The *Bulletin* exemplifies how IBI print materials created a continuum between internal work and public accountability, and conveyed IPE's unwavering commitment to imagining and planning for the futures of Black children and their families in the face of socioeconomic and

COLLEGE COMES TO THE BLACK COMMUNITY

OAK PARK SCHOOL OF AFRO - AMERICAN THOUGHT

3545 Sacramento Blvd.
Sacramento, California
457 - 1618

FIGURE I.3. Brochure from Oak Park School of Afro-American Thought. The interior lists the Summer 1969 / Fall 1969 / Spring 1970 course offerings developed by The Black Student Union of Sacramento City College. Source: Shule Jumamose Archive.

educational obstacles specific to Black people and Black communities. Signals about the education of Black children in 2020 mirrored stories and patterns of Black parents turning to nonmainstream alternatives with the same rationales that had motivated IPE visionaries and other Black institution builders to establish IBIs in the 1960s and 1970s: systemic racism, racist ideas, and lack of (or only partial access to) robust educational opportunities for Black children.[17] I began to think of Black institution builders, including the IPE work council photographed at the table, as futurists who were forecasting for Black lives—they were mapping out what future generations of Black children and their families would need to have and leverage more agency in their lives. However, the more I learned about Black institution builders' publications and lives through oral history interviews, the more I realized these leaders were doing more than forecasting: they were futuring.

I define *futuring* as intentional collective planning and future making—prioritizing, reflecting, and seeking to spark innovation, sustainability, and opportunities for Black self-determination across and through the domains of education, wellness, and economic prosperity. Forecasting is transactional and primarily an individual endeavor, sometimes characterized as getting "there" early ("there" standing in for the future). Futuring, on the other hand, is relational and distinctly values arriving *as a collective*.[18] IPE publications, especially the *Bulletin*, like other print material created, produced, and disseminated by IBIs, are historical beacons that can be read as highly relevant maps of/for the future. I explore and center these publications as tools useful as signals for the future of Black education and for shaping future-oriented pedagogies.

Black Books Bulletin and the Chicago Black Arts Continuum

Launched in 1971, IPE's *Bulletin* emerged at the intersection of Amiri Baraka's "It's Nation Time" and Madhubuti's assertion that art was not for "art's sake" but for "people's sake."[19] The Black Arts Movement is often described as beginning in 1965, when poet LeRoi Jones, one of the few Black poets with membership in the famed Beat Poets from Greenwich Village, made his pilgrimage to Harlem after the assassination of Malcolm X. In Harlem, he became Imamu Amiri Baraka and established the Black Arts Repertory Theatre/School.

Some might say that Chicago was already entrenched in a Black Arts Movement prior to Baraka's well-documented transition to uptown New York. Home to an ecosystem of Black-led artistic and intellectual endeavors, Chicago's Black Renaissance was flowering in the 1930s. Dr. Margaret Taylor-Burroughs was instrumental in establishing the South Side Community Art Center and later she and her husband, Charles Burroughs, and other colleagues established the Ebony Museum of Negro History (now the DuSable Black History Museum and Education Center) initially in their South Side Chicago home. Chicago also had had its share of Black-owned newspapers—something I discuss further in Chapter 1. In her "third person memoir of Lorraine Hansberry," Imani Perry notes, "the Chicago Black Press was robust," creating a culture where "a crop of young writers" could both publish and "flourish."[20] Indeed, the

Bulletin was in a long line of Black publications. Poets and writers were already publishing in the *Negro Digest*, established in November 1942 by Johnson Publishing Company and later edited by Hoyt Fuller, who oversaw its transition to *Black World* in 1971, using its pages as a literary arts pathway to engage in intellectual debates about issues impacting Black people globally. Fuller published new voices in poetry such as Haki Madhubuti, and Madhubuti interviewed Fuller for the inaugural issue of the *Bulletin*. IPE visionaries saw themselves as part of a larger constellation of Black creativity and institution building in Chicago.

A recent exhibit at the Oakland Museum of California, *Angela Davis: Seize the Time*, featured an interview in which Davis posited that music, poetry, and visual arts have the power to reach people and spark activism more than "didactic conversations."[21] My father shared something similar, from the vantage point of everyday folks who engaged in Black institution building in the 1970s, such as he and my mother: "We wanted to be literate. We wanted to be educated. People who were not poets started writing and speaking poetically because poets taught us how to speak to audiences. What better force than a poet to say things we would not dare say?"[22] Attuned to this truth, Hoyt Fuller, Conrad Kent Rivers, and Gerald McWorter (Abdul Alkalimat), established the Organization of Black American Culture in 1966; Madhubuti was a member. With other Chicago artists, the Organization of Black American Culture designed and executed the Wall of Respect, a collection of murals and verse on 43rd and Langley Avenue that served as a site for performance art and organizing. Pulitzer Prize–winning poet Gwendolyn Brooks and jazz musician Oscar Brown Jr. worked with youth from the Blackstone Rangers gang on a performance piece entitled "Opportunity, Please Knock." Collectives such as AFRICOBRA (African Commune of Bad Relevant Artists), Kuumba Theatre Workshop, and the Communiversity offered Black Chicagoans opportunities to engage in an array of artistic and intellectual endeavors.

IPE expanded these institution-building efforts, which had the foresight to center children and education. Rejecting 1975 as the typically identified end of the Black Arts Movement, Madhubuti asserts, "for me it has never stopped." Third World Press remained the nation's oldest independent Black publishing house, and Black children were still being educated in IPE's African-centered preschool when I started writing this book.[23] Just as it is important to reflect on Madhubuti's assertion that the Black Arts Movement did not end in 1975, I must underscore that building independent Black educational institutions did not begin in the 1960s. These efforts are part of the enduring legacy of people of African descent seeking literacy and education. Historian James Anderson's groundbreaking study *The Education of Blacks in the South, 1860–1935* dispels the mythology of Northern missionaries being the sole providers of an education infrastructure for newly freed Blacks. Anderson posits when Northern missionaries arrived in the South, some found themselves "astonished, and later chagrined, to discover many ex-slaves had established their own educational collectives and associations, staffed schools entirely with Black teachers, and were unwilling to allow their education movement to be controlled by 'civilized' Yankees."[24] In his foreword to Mwalimu Shujaa's book *Too Much Schooling, Too Little Education: A Paradox of Black Life in White Societies*, Haki Madhubuti references Anderson's historiography and calls his findings foundational to the work of Black institution builders of the 1960s and 1970s. Madhubuti asserts that Anderson "makes it clear that African Americans viewed education as birthright in the same light as freedom," despite efforts to diminish Black people's efforts to access literacy and learning.[25] Ultimately, Shujaa's edited volume troubles the assumption that "education" is part and parcel of attending school, especially for people of African descent in the United States. "African-centered thinking," according to Shujaa, "brings with it the responsibility for changing oppressive social conditions." Ultimately, this mindset seeks to contribute to the "betterment of humanity."[26]

IPE's enduring commitment to the collective can be seen on pages of the *Bulletin*, where visionaries wrestled with issues salient to Black people "wherever they may be," with a keen eye for developing a literate and literary citizenry.[27] IPE visionaries put their "stake in the stream"—to borrow from Soyini Walton—in Chicago, but the *Bulletin* was designed to demonstrate how challenges in that city were linked to struggles for Black liberation around the globe. Here, I assert that the "potential" and "possibility" for thriving Black futures is what makes examination of IBIs valuable to contemporary debates in education that pertain to Black children, Black families, and Black communities. IBIs are intermediaries between African and Black pasts, present, and futures.

Historiography for the Future: Notes on Methodology

At first glance, this study might be viewed as historical ethnography. I do consider the "lived world of participants" and put participants into conversation with primary source documents.[28] While I uncover stories and patterns from the Black Arts Movement via historical ethnography, analysis of Shule Jumamose Archive documents, and oral history interviews with IPE visionaries and artists whose work was included in the *Bulletin*, my work is also guided by foresight methods and futures thinking. Foresight refers to the capacity for humans, in "a systematic way," to "imagine and engage with alternative futures and to then identify those futures which need to be shaped, nurtured and felt in the present"[29] Foresight may seem like a misplaced concept in a historiography of IBIs, yet IPE visionaries were futurists who paid close attention to trends or signals in education, leveraged these to chart a new path for Black children and families, and prioritized the education and well-being of Black children in all they did to ensure that future generations of Black families would have access to self-determined futures.

In her 2018 introduction to *How Long 'til Black Future Month?* (also the essay's original title), author N. K. Jemison distilled the freedom and value of community-level futures visioning and articulation, stating: "How terrifying it's been to realize no one thinks my people have a future and how gratifying to finally accept myself and begin spinning futures I want to see."[30] In a similar vein, Haki Madhubuti recalls reading Alvin Toffler's *Future Shock* (1970) and being introduced to the concept of telecommuting, which he did between Chicago and Howard University in Washington, DC, where he was a writer-in-residence in the 1970s.[31] In the late 1960s and 1970s, IPE visionaries and Black institution builders throughout the United States similarly began to articulate and take action around futures *they* wanted to see for Black children and families, transitioning very intentionally from *reacting* to established white institutions that isolated or excluded them altogether to *reimagining* how IBIs could focus on the needs and desires of Black people in ways that would cultivate and sustain their self-determination and self-reliance.

Prior to the pandemic, I embarked on a futures journey, participating in a foresight and design thinking training. My intention was to learn from and with so-called futurists as I conceptualized a Futures Matter pedagogical stance for those who seek equitable and justice possibilities and future norms in US schools.[32] For the workshop, I drafted an outline of a futures project entitled "What Is the Future of Black Children in Schools?" My intended focus on schools became stifling, though, as it was difficult to imagine schools, as currently configured, having the capacity to foment expansive futures for Black children. One of the first tasks in the foresight process is to "look back to look ahead," gathering historical context for the future you are imagining. Throughout my work to imagine the future of Black children through the pathways of education, I kept returning to the work of IBIs and Black institution builders in the 1960s and 1970s. What lessons could educators learn from these institution builders and how could their past efforts help us imagine and establish justice- and equity-oriented institutions in the present?

Many IBIs in the early 1970s focused on the whole child and their families, including with respect to overall wellness, engagement with arts and literary arts, and agency or self-determination. IBIs provided what is currently referred to as wraparound services, providing opportunities for intergenerational learning for children, their caregivers, and the larger community. With robust focus on defining the purpose of education—and pathways to fulfill this purpose—IBIs and their leaders were future-oriented, considering outcomes several generations out.

By the end of my foresight training, my question had decentered schools and schooling.[33] I instead asked, "What is the future of education for Black children?" and "What is the future of Black education?" Due to this lens work and tool application, I now refer to my work as Historiography for the Future, that is, methodological intervention that engages historical writings and memories while seeking to (re)create maps for the future. Historiography for the Future suggests that histories and futures not only intersect but should be actively and simultaneously considered when we reflect on and explore contemporary issues in the education of Black children. Inspired by Futures methodologies, Afrofuturism, retrofuturism, and what Robin D. G. Kelley refers to as future-oriented historiography, I position Black institution builders as futurists forecasting for Black lives by planning and building a world that did not yet exist.[34] IPE founders, for example, could be considered early Afrofuturists; they were not only challenging the omission of Black people from the social, political, economic, and education fabric of America's story but also proactively dreaming and forming institutions focused on Black life and Black freedom.

In many ways, the Shule Jumamose Archive serves as a portal between the history, present, and future of Black education. Hidden in plain sight in my childhood home, these materials beget the question, Where are Black archives waiting to be unearthed in family homes throughout the United States? One aim of my Historiography for the Future work is to bring forth ways to humanize research, cultivate "citizen archivists," and make histories such as the story of IBIs accessible so everyday people can locate themselves, their values, their families, and their communities within larger narratives of Black education. *Futuring Black Lives* seeks to inspire citizen archivists to seek out maps and mapping tools that their families may hold, and to consider multiple pathways forward. These "ideas in unexpected places" have transformative potential in charting Black educational futures.[35]

From Fugitivity to Futuring: Situating the Book

Historical research in American education suggests that to gain full(er) understanding(s) of the education and intellectual traditions of Black people, we locate both "forgotten readers" and "the new literate and literary."[36] *Futuring Black Lives* is part of the enduring legacy of Black tradition recovery, surfacing untapped histories of Black people's distinct and undeterred quest to educate themselves, their children, and their communities. IBIs have consistently informed and embodied the literate and literary aspirations of Black Americans—and centered reading, writing, thinking, and doing as foundations for planning and pursuing desired futures. In addition to being in dialogue with Anderson and Shujaa's work, *Futuring Black Lives* seeks to engage with historiography in the tradition of Vanessa Siddle Walker's *Their Highest Potential: An African American School Community in the Segregated South* (1996) and *The Lost Education of Horace Tate: Uncovering the Hidden Heroes Who Fought for Justice in Schools* (2018). I see my notion of historical signals as akin to Siddle Walker's notion of "historical ideas"; both see historiography as an opportunity to grapple with current education issues impacting Black children in contemporary settings.

In many ways, IBIs and *Futuring Black Lives* sit at the intersection of education research and Black Studies, an intersection kihana m. ross and Jarvis Givens refer to as "the clearing" or "Black Education Studies."[37] These scholars note that the "kinship between Black Studies and education studies is historical in nature," and that both are "problem-oriented interdisciplinary fields" with the potential to offer new discourse for how we talk about and imagine Black education. Illuminating the "commitments" in this proposed field, I posit that Black Education Studies is a futuring project, given its focus on "the needs of Black youth among us and those yet to be born . . . committed to Black educational futurities where collective flourishing and dignity are the norm rather than exception."[38] *Futuring Black Lives* carries this commitment by upholding the intellectual traditions of Black Studies while maintaining pedagogical commitments to equity and transformative justice in education. Givens demonstrates how Black educators in the nineteenth century engaged in "fugitive pedagogy" that simultaneously "contested ideas of black inferiority" and imagined "black freedom."[39]

Fugitivity and futuring converge in the idea that pedagogy, in the context of Black education, is in service of future(s) visioning. Futuring, in the case of IBIs and the work of the Black Arts Movement, centered the collective work of Black people worldwide who may or may not have been recognized as educators formally, but who understood their role as influencers of their children and children in their community. To envision and create responsive institutions that addressed the needs and desires of Black people, Black institution builders looked to and beyond Black American scholars to frame key issues. The leaders of newly independent Black countries offered numerous learnings about the tedious nature of rebuilding institutions with Black people's freedom in mind. Jitu Weusi, co-founder of The East and Uhuru Sasa Shule (Freedom Now School), explained, "After [Carter G.] Woodson, you didn't have directions. You didn't know where to go. [Julius] Nyerere helped us understand where to go."[40] Black institution builders in the late 1960s and early 1970s used these points of reference to generate and operationalize futuring ideas, in the form of schools, learning communities, food cooperatives, printing presses, and publications that could transcend—and have transcended—those institutions' immediate reach and tenure.

Finally, *Futuring Black Lives* builds on the arc of research examining Black education in Chicago and the contributions of Black institution builders at the micro level. I consider Elizabeth Todd-Breland's *A Political Education: Black Politics and Education Reform in Chicago since the 1960s* (2018) and Worth Kamili Hayes's *Schools of Our Own: Chicago's Golden Age of Black Private Education* (2020) as foundational to this work. Todd-Breland examined the roles and work of Black teachers in Chicago's school reform efforts, and Hayes provides a historical landscape of education alternatives to public schools for Black families in Chicago including some treatment of IPE. Both scholars highlight the need for further excavation to locate and learn from maps of the future of Black education by demonstrating the nuanced and valuable work of Black educators and Black education in prior eras.

Outline of This book

Futuring Black Lives begins with macro-level examination of Black institution builders during the Black Arts Movement, noting that many of these leaders advocated Black Cultural Nationalism, the belief that African ways of knowing and being traveled with them during their violent removal and disbursement through the Transatlantic slave trade, and that these ways of knowing were subsequently incubated throughout Diasporic communities across and beyond the United States. In an influential study of independent Black educational institutions, *We Are an African People: Independent Education, Black Power, and The Radical Imagination* (2016), Russell Rickford offers a macro-analysis of IBIs throughout the United States. Yet Black Arts Movement scholars have also called for examination of regional and local projects of that era. The Black aesthetic that defined the arts domain during this period did strongly influence IBI visionaries and builders, and Chapter 1, "What About Our Tomorrows?: Institution Building for Black Lives," introduces publications and ephemera produced by the institutions they created. I consider how IBIs self-positioned and wanted to be viewed by those on the outside looking in, often including other institution builders and certainly the Black people they hoped would support them. Chapter 1 raises another possible lens through which to view the focal archival materials. What if these materials map/ped journeys to the future? How might the creators of these materials have been thinking about their longevity and temporality to bridge the past, present, and future of Black self-determination? This first chapter grounds the Institute of Positive Education and *Black Books Bulletin* as part of a larger constellation of dreamers and doers giving shape to institutions within and beyond Chicago.

Chapter 2, "'We Are Studying to Advance the Struggle': IPE Visionaries Forecasting for Black Lives," invites readers into the stories of IPE's co-founders, creators, teachers, and visionaries. Drawing from oral history interviews, this chapter highlights the lived experiences of several IPE visionaries including Haki Madhubuti, Carol D. Lee, Soyini Walton, Jabari Mahiri, and Kimya and considers how personal context informed the work they chose to do collectively on behalf of Black children and their families. I deploy *visionaries* not to elevate IPE co-founders over other Black institution builders but to invoke their strategic orientation toward the future. In this chapter I am purposeful about capturing the experiences of IPE visionaries—women and men—to challenge the Black Arts Movement narratives that center one hero (typically male).[41] This is not to say that IPE did not experience challenges with gender equity. The women I interviewed did not name gender equity as a concern or a challenge; they focused on their work with Black children, in education, and in communities that was necessary then and now. It is important to note this is not an exhaustive list of everyone who was involved in either co-founding or working with IPE; other untapped experiences are not represented here. For example, I was unable to interview Johari Amini, a co-founder of IPE and "cultural mother" to visionaries. All the same, the visionaries featured here were involved in different aspects of imagining a future for Black children and their families.[42] In this chapter, I repurpose forecasting tools typically reserved for businesses planning, to build corporate wealth, in pursuit of an altogether different asset: Black children whose education and well-being have been prioritized and cultivated as imaginings and pursuits of thriving futures.

If IPE visionaries were forecasting for Black lives and engaging in formal acts of futuring, one of their primary tools was the quarterly literary journal *Black Books Bulletin*, published between 1971 and 1981. Chapter 3, "Between 'Precariousness' and 'Possibility': The Emergence of *Black Books Bulletin*," examines how IPE sought to leverage their journal to engage literary imagination in conversations about Black Cultural Nationalism and Pan-Africanism. Here, I also examine some of the tensions between and among educators and Black Nationalists to demonstrate how IPE was able to use their journal to hold itself and the community accountable for their commitments and actions in Chicago's Black community. The *Bulletin* provided temporality to IPE's efforts to demonstrate the past (Identity), present (Purpose), and future (Direction) as a continuum and as a circle.

The Black Power and Black Arts Movements spurred the creation of several publications throughout the United States in the 1960s and 1970s. Some focused on research and scholarship, including *The Black Scholar*, established by Robert Chrisman and Nathan Hare in 1969 in San Francisco; *The Cricket* (*Black Music in Evolution*), created by Amiri Baraka in Newark, New Jersey, also in 1968; and *Nkombo*, created by New Orleans–based poets and writers Tom Dent and Kalamu ya Salaam in 1968, primarily with focus on the arts. Drawing from *Negro Digest / Black World*, edited by Hoyt Fuller, Madhubuti imagined a journal dedicated to "Black ideas," to include reviews of literature written by, for, and about Black people that offered direction and scholarship in education, history, and psychology. The *Bulletin* sought to be an "influencer"; that is, IPE used the journal's pages to offer positive and affirming images and words to nourish Black families. To this end, the *Bulletin* served (and can continue to serve) as a portal between histories and futures while anchoring readers in the sociopolitical landscape of the 1970s, which required Black leaders and caregivers alike to anticipate obstacles and pathways to self-determination for themselves and their families and communities.

One of the *Bulletin*'s recurring sections, "Books for the Young," featured reviews of children's literature that the editorial team considered useful for nation building and self-determination, or, on the flip side, detrimental to Black children's identity development. Chapter 4, "'There Is No Magic . . . Except the Magic of Truth': Nation Building with Books for the Young" examines the role of children's literature, the implicit values surrounding the cultivation of young Black readers, and how literature could be in service of teaching children worldbuilding skills. "Books for the Young" encapsulated IPE's views on "correct Black education," organized around the design principles of Identity, Purpose, and Direction and offering tangible tools for adult influencers to co-construct desired community and world norms with and for children. This focus on cultivating the next generation of Black readers, writers, and thinkers distinguishes the *Bulletin* from other publications during this time, which IPE visionaries noted in their interviews.

The final chapter, "'The Present Passes . . . the Next Day—Mars,'" connects the work of IPE visionaries and other Black institution builders to contemporary conversations regarding the education of Black children in the United States. Rather than "lessons learned" or "implications," I offer values espoused by IPE visionaries that can serve as a compass for new work imagining the future of Black education. In this chapter, I reflect on relevant scaffolding already available from the thinking and outputs of independent Black institution builders. In addition, Chapter 5 offers a vision for Historiography for the Future as a conceptual tool for Black Educational studies and shows readers how and why forecasting and futuring provide valuable opportunities to imagine worlds that do not yet exist and create plans to realize those futures.

CHAPTER 1

"What About Our Tomorrows?"

Institution Building for Black Lives

When IPE outgrew its first home, two storefronts on South Ellis, the institution's leaders set their sights on a well-worn, unoccupied building owned by the Catholic church across the street. According to Haki Madhubuti, the broker representing the Archdiocese did not want to sell him the building because he considered Madhubuti "too radical." Madhubuti tapped friends who were part of the Catholic community. They recommended he reach out to Bishop Wilton Gregory, a respected African American bishop on the South Side of Chicago. After calling Bishop Gregory's office several times, leaving the name "Haki Madhubuti," Madhubuti decided to use his birth name, "Don L. Lee." Retelling this story, Madhubuti highlights Bishop Gregory's assistant asking, "Are you the poet?" before scheduling his fifteen-minute meeting. He recounts meeting the bishop and bringing Third World Press books and IPE materials to share—a practice he continues today—and the fifteen-minute meeting became a two-hour conversation. Bishop Gregory wrote a letter of support for Madhubuti's purchase of the unused building; however, the letter was only the first step.[1] IPE needed a $50,000 down payment. Madhubuti and his wife, Carol D. Lee, took out a second mortgage on their home for $40,000, and IPE's board voted to commit $10,000 to purchase the rectory, the parking lot, and the building that currently houses the New Concept School and Betty Shabazz International Charter School.

"It's always a struggle but it's our struggle," Madhubuti declared, when recounting their acquisition story with me.[2] Soyini Walton, IPE visionary, co-founder, and later principal of IPE's Betty Shabazz International Charter School, asserted, "Space and a mortgage makes you a real revolutionary," when talking about IPE's longevity in the community and ownership of space.[3] Indeed, IPE's investment in brick and mortar was tethered to their vision for the future. To be in the "ideas business"—to borrow from Madhubuti—a lab, a studio, and space to imagine and to map the future were needed. Recalling early days when IPE visionaries had to find spaces to hold meetings and events, Madhubuti noted that most of the Black-owned buildings were owned by churches, and "When you are operating out of churches and using their buildings . . . if you say the wrong thing then you have to go." IPE was a Pan-African organization with Black Cultural Nationalist leanings, and values that did not always align with the goals of Black churches:

> Well, the problem we were growing up with is the church is always talking about the life after death. What was bothering me all the time was like, "What about our tomorrows? What are we going to do for ourselves that will allow us to have a stake in the future?" It doesn't matter where [Black people] are . . . we need to [have] a stake in the future. My question to all these people who say they're working for black people is, "What do you own?" I'm not talking about your suits and your cars. I am talking about your home. If you own your own home that's a part of it . . . the only thing that nobody nowhere is making any more of is land. It's land. Okay?[4]

Noting that "the Black church remained the most powerful single institution in terms of wealth and mass support," in their influential study of Black life in Chicago in 1945, St. Claire Drake and Horace R. Cayton assert that "the pulpit was the main source of news and inspiration . . . the minister was publicist as well as exhorter . . . but the Negro press emerged as a victorious competitor."[5] Chicago's first Black newspaper, *The Conservator*, established in 1878, had opened the gates for others to follow. When Robert S. Abbott's *The Chicago Defender* published its first issue in 1905, Abbott's "genius," according to Ethan Michaeli, "was to create a newspaper that could simultaneously offer news for the Pullman porter as well as the social climber, the 'Race Man,' and the businessman."[6] Decades later, Third World Press and IPE's acquisition of a church rectory to house new "Black ideas," with a keen eye for Black "tomorrows," held some irony, given that many IBI leaders may have named "Blackness" *as* their religion. Or perhaps we can better understand the situation as poetic; whereas Black churches focused on "life after death," IBIs were focused on helping Black people desire, imagine, and plan their lived "tomorrows."

So how did Black institution builders from the Black Power and Black Arts Movements create infrastructure through which Black people might have "stake in the future" and, to borrow from Soyini Walton, put their "stake in the stream?" Imagining and planning for collective "tomorrows," which I refer to as futuring, requires a mindset, value system, and way of knowing and being. Black futuring in the 1960s and 1970s also required tangible tools, including a brick-and-mortar presence—a space people could walk into and sit down in to think, dream, and collaborate without restrictions on their speech, ideas, or time. For IPE and other IBIs, investment in Black print culture provided a viable mechanism for the less tangible acts of futuring, as well as tangible outputs of that work. Books, pamphlets, journals, newspapers, magazines, and other print matter provided material that could nourish and sustain ideas and shared language, while simultaneously creating a permanent record of words that could be put to work and have longevity beyond their authors or any physical building.

This chapter explores how Black institution builders leveraged print culture to introduce themselves, their institutions, and their work, while creating a record of their efforts. I begin this discussion by contextualizing the work of IPE and IBIs within a larger conversation of Black literate lives and how IPE's institution-building efforts were shaped by local context. Next, I consider how Black print culture provided opportunities for Black institution builders to introduce themselves, their values, and their ideology, especially in the areas of education, community, and family. To do this, I focus on three pamphlets/publications that represent local institution-building efforts in different parts of the United States: *Planning an Independent Black Educational Institution*, published as part of the Congress of African People's September 1970 convening in Atlanta; *Outline for a New African Educational Institution: The Uhuru Sasa School Program*, published by The East in Brooklyn; and Ahidiana Work/Study Center *Operating Principles*, a book published by their type-setting company, Ahidiana-Habari, in New Orleans.

How did these IBI-produced publications provide concrete examples of the Seven Principles of Blackness, also known as Kwanzaa—with an emphasis on the principles of Self-Determination (Kujichagulia), Collective Work & Responsibility (Ujima), and Cooperative Economics (Ujamaa)—not only to create an infrastructure for schools but also for other businesses? I draw from poet, writer, and institution builder Kalamu ya Salaam's proposed "local/national/local model," or L/N/L. Salaam's model suggests beginning one's understanding of the Black Arts Movement and institution building with community-driven efforts in neighborhoods and cities, connecting this work with efforts unfolding at the national level, and returning to the local context. I use this model for examining the Black Arts Movement as an organizing principle for this chapter.

Black Arts Movement scholar James Smethurst leveraged Salaam's Black Arts Movement theory-building model in asserting that the movement "started out as disparate local initiatives across a wide geographic area, coalescing into a national movement with a sense of broader coherence that, in turn, inspired more local, grassroots activities."[7] I similarly begin with IPE's local institution-building efforts before turning to examples in other regions documented in publications produced and disseminated by IBIs. I keep in mind that many Black institution builders during the Black Power and Black Arts Movements were poets, writers, and scholars (some working toward graduate degrees while engaging in this work) who knew full well the power of documenting their activities and archiving their ideas for future generations. Their cartography detailed the social and political context in which they created innovative structures and ensured that their futuring work would endure via Black print culture.[8] While most of the materials referenced in this chapter are part of the Shule Jumamose Archive, which serves as praxis for Historiography for the Future, other archival materials provide evidence of institution building *not* captured in the Shule Jumamose Archive, demonstrating how important it is to put the archive into conversation with other primary sources. With respect to the three focal publications of this chapter, I first came across the *Planning* document in the University of California, Davis Library's Special Collections and saw it again at the Schomburg Center for Research on Black Culture, in the Preston Wilcox Papers. The *Outline* is a part of the Shule Jumamose Archive and includes highlights and annotations by my father. Ahidiana's *Operating Principles* is part of their co-founders' ambitious Ahidiana Remembrance site, an online archive that includes a range of materials produced by Ahidiana between 1973 and 1988.[9]

In this chapter, I ultimately seek to generate dialogue regarding what it means to be a "citizen archivist" and reclaim artifacts that are sometimes hiding in plain sight, in family homes and in spaces owned and occupied by local organizations and institutions. Materials in the Shule Jumamose Archive were originally acquired to inspire and inform my parents and their colleagues as they embarked on their own institution-building efforts. The reason the contents were later curated and preserved by my father, though, was his belief that they possess enduring lessons on developing Black children's Identity, Purpose, and Direction and that these materials would continue to have value beyond the moments and movements that spurred the creation and operation of Shule Jumamose. Indeed, one of my goals for Historiography for the Future is to leverage IBI futuring efforts to inform and possibly advance plans and designs for equity in contemporary institutions of education.

"We Could Not Have Survived": Contextualizing the Work of IPE

The word "institution" can conjure images of buildings and bureaucracy and, for some, a sense of isolation and/or exclusion. Derived from the Latin word *institutus* or "to set up; put in place; arrange; found; establish; appoint; designate; govern; administer; teach, instruct," *institution* is defined as "an established organization or corporation . . . especially of public character."[10] Black institution builders during the Black Power and Black Arts movements understood the power of institutions to "validate knowledge, help to shape vision, inculcate values, and provide the foundation for community stability."[11] Notably, Carol D. Lee's reflection on establishing IPE, "African-centered education at work," revealed the intentionality behind establishing an institution and using "Institute" as part of its name.[12]

In the context of Black living and futuring for Black lives, institutions have played a key role in organizing for freedom, education, and justice, though some such institutions lack (or have lacked) a formal building. Elsewhere, I have examined how writers, poets, speakers, and "doers of the word" have formed collectives to engage in literate and literary practices. The twenty-first-century participatory literacy communities I have documented often note that their gathering in the name of poetry, writing, reading, and exchanging ideas was "not new," a nod to the history of "forgotten readers," including enslaved people of African descent who continued to pursue literate lives despite severe and violent consequences.[13] Participatory literacy communities also acknowledge that the spaces they have curated, whether in formal buildings or at someone's kitchen table, are "institutions within themselves."[14]

At the time IPE was established, in 1969, Third World Press was two years into publishing the works of Black poets, writers, scholars, and practitioners. When IPE decided to publish their quarterly literary journal, *Black Books Bulletin*, in 1971, Black Chicago was grappling with the "Daley Machine," Richard J. Daley's twenty-one-year reign as mayor, and "Boss" politics rendered much of the Black community disconnected from the larger city.[15] When I interviewed IPE visionaries, they seldom—if ever—referenced what was happening politically in Chicago, not because they were not politically astute or engaged but because they chose to focus on what they could build, shape, and create for Black people. Black Power and Black Arts Movement stakeholders viewed themselves as building a "nation within a nation."[16] In the context of Chicago, a "city within a city" may have been a more accurate lens.[17] IBI publications elsewhere similarly demonstrated how Black life often operated in/as its own "city," as seen on the pages of *The Black Panther* (established in Oakland, California, in 1967), *Unity & Struggle* (initially *Black NewArk*, established in Newark, New Jersey, in 1968), and *Black News* (established in Brooklyn, New York, in 1969).

Today, scholars are beginning to reframe Black people's relationships to their cities by reimagining cities as sites of possibility and centering overlooked spaces excavated by artists, activists, and everyday people. In the case of Chicago, "the image of 'broad shoulders'" or narratives of "an industrial city too brash, or a postindustrial city too defeated to dream" long rendered Black institution builders' innovation and acts of futuring at the local level invisible, in much of the literature.[18] However, in a compelling analysis of "chocolate cities," Marcus Anthony Hunter and Zandria F. Robinson argue that "our current maps of Black life are wrong" and call for active reframing using an "asset-based approach."[19] IPE and all its entities—including a school, literary journal, and gathering space for intergenerational teaching and learning—were proactive sites of possibility created by visionaries who, "rather than simply complain and react," chose, according to co-founder Carol D. Lee, a "proactive stance, defining within a community context the possibilities and gifts that Black children offer the world, and creating institutions to manifest its ideals."[20]

Lee notes that IPE was not alone in these endeavors:

> One of the things we formed very much in Chicago, not just with [IPE] and the school, but all the various institutional frames that were going on ... just a lot of institution building going on at that time. And we were all centered in a fundamental belief that we were persons of African descent, that we inherited traditions and knowledge that had sustained our people over the generations from our ancestors. And that we had a responsibility to pass that on to the next generation. And so [IPE] would always have naming ceremonies. Hannibal Afrik did the naming ceremony for all three of our children. And what we understood from the naming ceremony, it wasn't really about giving a child a name as much as it was about introducing a child to a community.[21]

In many ways, reference to Hannibal Afrik (Harold Charles) affirms the interconnectedness of Chicago's Black institution-building networks. Afrik established Shule Ya Watoto on the west side of Chicago in 1972, around the same time IPE was developing their African-centered preschool as a full-time program. Lee and Afrik were educator-activists in Operation Breadbasket, and Lee described Afrik and others as part of this community who felt shared responsibility for the "next generation."[22]

While IPE visionaries always had a sense that Chicago's Black artists were at the forefront of the Black Arts Movement and establishing Black institutions, art history long discounted Chicago's Black Arts Movement. Recent scholarship, however, has reclaimed Chicago's role as "the hub" of this period, wherein a "thriving visual arts scene gave visual form to the movement and confronted its own specific challenges."[23] These "specific challenges" are what make examinations of local manifestations of the Black Arts Movement important. IPE visionaries like Kimya Moyo had a strong sense of the institution's place in the larger constellation of IBIs nationwide:

> So, when you talk about back in the '70s at [IPE], it wasn't solely [IPE]. It was also the Jeff Donaldsons and the Murry DePillars. The artists that were involved. It was the poets. It was the musicians. It was all those restaurants that provided venues for these poets to come. Where were we going to enjoy ourselves? Where can we go see a Gil Scott-Heron and be uplifted? So none of this is stuff is out there separate, standing as an island by itself. It's all connected because we all need each other. We could not have survived. That's the institution building.[24]

Moyo understood Black institution building to operate on both a continuum and across domains. She noted that the two artists who made up Chicago's AFRICOBRA (African Commune of Bad Relevant Artists) were inspired by Jeff Donaldson's call for Black artists to view themselves as a collective creating work for their community.[25] Black Arts Movement poets, writers, and artists, such as Haki Madhubuti, used their work and reach to not only illuminate issues Black people were facing but to strategize how to build institutions that would intervene in sustainable ways:

> We have a mechanism . . . institutional structures that answer the key questions about life that we provide, not what other people provide, but what we provide, and that's what we have tried to do all of my life. . . . And so we try to put all of our resources, our monies, into building these institutional structures, which turns out at one level to be your legacy also, but I'm a poet. You know what I'm saying? I'm a poet.[26]

Poets during the Black Arts Movement were not merely wordsmiths. Nor were they simply penning ideas and waiting for their next poetry reading. Black poets, writers, and artists were using their words, sounds, and power to organize people and invite deep reflection on what it meant to build a legacy. Answering "key questions about life" needed the precision, intentionality, and vision of poets. Moyo, who served as one of IPE's lead math educators, drew the connections between arts and institution building:

> So you have to be about futuring. You have to see if your lens is not wide enough.... Then the job is to expand the lens. What is our job? Our job is to expand the lens for us today, so that we can understand the impact that we are making. When Haki, when Kalamu ya Salaam can write poems on self-determination, that's major because then that's something that people, even if they don't know the whole poem, then there's something, there's a phrase or something that's catchy that's going to make them recognize self-determination. Something about that is important. So all our poets, all our musicians, there's no disconnect. They're all related.[27]

Madhubuti, for example, specifically leveraged his stature *as* a poet to pen essays on education and institution building that provided guidelines for new approaches to and experiences of Black education. Inspired by Mwalimu Julius Nyerere, president of Tanzania and an educator, Madhubuti emphasized that educators for Black children had to "be responsible and responsive to their *own needs*" (his emphasis), noting that otherwise Black children would be taught, in mainstream schooling, to serve needs beyond their community "at the expense and detriment" of Black people.[28]

For IBI visionaries, "correct Black education" required values and mindsets that acknowledged Black pasts, the socio-political climate of the present, and dreams and plans for future generations of Black children. To understand the shared commitments and vision of Black institution builders during of the late 1960s and early 1970s, in the context of a post-civil-rights or long-civil-rights era, messaging from their own publications is particularly salient. With their own typesetting and publishing companies, several IBIs could produce materials they believed to be relevant and urgent in a timely manner. Looking at some such materials, I next examine how Black institution builders provided maps for/to liberatory futures for Black people, with a focus on Black education as a critical priority.

"Education Is a Serious Business": IBIs Futuring for Education

Inspired by "West Coast models" of organizing that he had witnessed while teaching at San Francisco State in 1967, Black Arts Movement architect Amiri Baraka co-created the United Brothers in Newark during what would become that city's "Black revolt," a time of upheaval when Black people demanded more say in education, housing, and politics, amid ongoing tensions between law enforcement and Black residents.[29] While the initial group was composed only of men, "dedicated Black women" formed its "core," with Amiri Baraka's wife, Amina Baraka, critical in organizing the United Sisters.[30] Recent scholarship has rightly centered the work of women in the Black Power and Black Arts movements, and historian Ashley Farmer asserts that the United Sisters' work was critical to the education platform developed with the United Brothers under an umbrella organization called the Committee for a Unified Newark.[31] Building on Malauna Karenga's Seven Principles of Blackness, the Committee eventually transitioned from implementing Black Cultural Nationalism locally, in Newark, to national reach through the Congress of African People. In fact, Madhubuti's classic text, *From Plan to Planet Life Studies: The Need for Afrikan Minds and Institutions*, notes that while the Nguzo Saba / Seven Principles of Blackness "originated" with Karenga, it was Amiri Baraka who "reactivated and actioned" them "to near perfection."[32] IPE, like many IBIs throughout the United States, became a Congress of African People affiliate.

In August 1970, the California Association for Afro American Education hosted a meeting to discuss "converting traditional institutions" and "establishing new institutions" to focus on Black education.[33] Ideas generated at this meeting became starting points for further dialogue and design work a month later, when the Congress of African People convened a Labor Day weekend workshop in Atlanta in 1970. The "Education and

Black Students" convening was important for Black institution builders for a few key reasons. One was that "the Black nationalists had never before attracted so many black elected officials and civil rights leaders to a Pan-African summit."[34] "Black self-determination" was identified as the shared objective across organizations and institutions during the convening, and several workshops were dedicated solely to education. Values of collaborative nation building set the tone: "This workshop is about business; taking care of business. It's Nation Time, Labor for a Nation. The ideological position for this conference has been proposed. A copy of it is enclosed in your registration kit. Please read it carefully. Therefore, there is no need for 'philosophical and/or ideological raps.' Let us Pan-Africanize and nationalize ourselves through our behavior toward each other and as members of this workshop."[35]

Workshop participants created *Planning an Independent Black Educational Institution*, a twenty-nine-page booklet calling Black institution builders to imagine institutions and schools as more than "reactionary, anti-oppression programs":

> We cannot over-emphasize the need to clearly define institutional purposes and objectives. . . . *Education is a serious business*, and we must begin to view it as such. What we are talking about is our children's future, our community's future, and our nation's future. It is no longer sufficient to claim that white-controlled institutions are de-educating our children. It is no longer sufficient to claim that we can do a better job—*we must be about the business of doing that better job*. We must accept responsibility for educating our children and for developing their minds to the fullest potential.[36]

The tone was urgent and demanded accountability within the Black community. The future of Black children, the Black community, and the nation, according to the document, were inextricably linked to education. Evoking Carter G. Woodson's *Mis-Education of the Negro* (1933), workshop stakeholders exhorted Black people to cease blaming "white-controlled" schools for "de-educating" Black children. The publication favored discourse of personal responsibility, self-help, and even rather harsh clarification that no excuses should be allowed when it came to futuring for the next generations.

In keeping with the aim of the Congress of African People and its localized roots in the Committee for a Unified Newark, stakeholders from across the nation journeyed to Atlanta to work, not just talk. They came to learn from and with each other so they could return to their local contexts with a shared philosophical framework to build education institutions that met local needs and reflected local priorities. Agreement with Woodson's statement that in public schools "the thought of inferiority of the Negro is drilled in . . . in almost every class [one] enters and in almost every book [one] studies" provided the rationale for the work of Black institution builders and offered new vocabulary such as "de-educate" and "re-educate" to fuel calls for a paradigm shift in educating Black children.[37] In a planning workshop at Nairobi College in East Palo Alto, California, that preceded the 1970 convening, stakeholders posited that "the primary function of an IBI is to 'educate the pure,'" and "'to de-educate the contaminated.'"[38]

The Atlanta workshop was facilitated by community organizer and educator Preston Wilcox and the *Planning an Independent Black Educational Institution* document was edited by Frank Satterwhite. Satterwhite organized the publication like a manual, providing definitions of education, the purpose and objectives of education in the context of IBIs, and specific methods for executing the plan. He began the document with Wilcox's definition of education—which had guided workshop stakeholders:

> Education is an act; it is not a resolution. It is an event, not a description of it. It is the struggle, not the preparation for it. It combines thinking, feeling, and acting into a single whole. It is a human act. It respects the learner and frees the teacher to learn. It is a people-building, family-building, community-building, and a nation-building act—or else it is indoctrination, brainwashing, domination, and westernization. It places the major responsibility for learning on the learner himself. It vests the teacher with the skill to foster liberation but not the skill to control. It is a human loving act between two people whose common destinies are bound together.[39]

For Wilcox and other Black institution builders, Black education ("thinking," "feeling," "acting") is the antithesis of a Western education ("indoctrination," "brainwashing," "domination"). Focus on building—people, family, and community—situates education as a verb, with stakeholders possessing agency to define the act of education. Also striking in this definition is the absence of hierarchy. Teachers are expected to create opportunities for learners to liberate themselves, and learners are viewed as having the ultimate responsibility for their liberation. Ultimately, the purpose and objectives of IBIs would be:

> (1) to provide African people with identity, purpose, and direction; and (2) to reinforce and perpetuate the ideology of the African World. Black people must know who they are and *that they are* (identity); know what to do and *why to do it* (purpose); know where to go and *how to get there* (direction). Thus, an IBI must develop an education program which directs and channels thoughts and patterns in addition to providing training to meet the needs of our people as we move toward freedom and independence.[40]

Planning, then, was a manual, a self-help book, a dictionary of new terms, and a map with signals and directions for institution builders at various stages of the institution-building process. While Wilcox's ideas were used to ground the document, reminders of the collective work of the Congress of African People's convening are echoed throughout the document.

"A Tool for Our Liberation:" Uhuru Sasa Shule

If *Planning an Independent Black Educational Institution* was a "how to" for Black institution builders, documenting the objectives, values, and ideology of Black education on a national scale, The East's *Outline for a New African Educational Institution: The Uhuru Sasa Shule Program* was an example of how IBIs leveraged print culture for local contexts. Established in 1969, The East was "a self-determining cultural and educational organization for African and African-descended people in central Brooklyn, New York" and the *Outline* document introduced Black families in Brooklyn and beyond to their Uhuru Sasa school program.[41] Issued by The East's publishing arm as part of their "Black Nation Education Series," opening pages of the *Outline* introduced Uhuru Sasa

Shule ("Freedom Now School") as a "young, developing African Education Institution" created "out of the need for African People to control the institution which equips us with skills, values, training necessary for the continued existence and further development of our race."[42] The *Outline* served multiple purposes: it provided a history of The East and all its entities, chronicled The East's decision to establish a school, and provided The East's definitions and philosophy of education and an overview of Uhuru Sasa's curriculum, parent expectations, and policies for staff.

Authored by The East's staff, led by New York educator Jitu Weusi (Les Campbell), this publication was positioned as an evaluative tool for their IBI, citing "extensive research" that went into preparing the document, in addition to "many hours . . . analysing our mistakes and successes."[43] Ultimately, the *Outline* sought to help other institution builders with their own local efforts. A copy in the Shule Jumamose Archives points to this; the section entitled "Our Philosophy of Education" bears red pencil notations in my father's handwriting, circling and underlining entire passages that might support institution building in California. Echoes of Woodson's concept of "mis-education" appear in the *Outline*, as occurred in the Congress of African People's *Planning* workshop document. Uhuru Sasa staff retell the story of African American students walking out of Franklin K. Lane school in November 1969, when New York's "Board of Miseducation" was "not about to allow Black youth an avenue to express their newfound Nationalism and racial pride."[44] This was not the first time The East's stakeholders employed the term "mis-education" in their indictment of New York's Department of Education; their newspaper, *Black News*, consistently substituted "education" with "mis-education" when any description involved the public school system.[45]

Weusi's own journey leaving the New York Department of Education was spurred when he witnessed both the courage of his students and the disciplinary action he received for taking them to a celebration of the life of Malcolm X.[46] Black teachers like Weusi sought to create a viable ecosystem to address the mis-education of Black children and engage parents in re-education processes, and this was why and how The East was established. Like IPE, The East was a Congress of African

People affiliate organization. Valuing student voice and agency, Uhuru Sasa staff echoed Wilcox's notion of education as a "human loving act" with teachers and learners sharing a vision for the future. The *Outline* introduced the African American Student Association as a "new breed of Black youth" holding adults in their lives accountable due to "their willingness to struggle and sacrifice."[47] Education was the portal through which The East's stakeholders could move from reacting to inequities in the US school system to reimagining what education for Black children could look, sound, and feel like. Weusi's featured essay in the *Bulletin*'s special issue on children and education noted that IBI schools that were initially an "angry reaction to educational genocide" of Black children needed to rebrand and retool from "temporary" to "permanent" institutions.[48] Karenga's Seven Principles of Blackness, according to the *Outline*, served as the foundation for The East's education programs and a tool for sustainability and permanence:

> We at Uhuru Sasa set as our educational goal the knowledge and practical application of the Seven Principles of Blackness. . . . The education provided must therefore encourage in each citizen the development of three things: an inquiring mind, an ability to learn from what others do, and reject or adapt it to his own needs and a basic confidence in his own position as a free and equal member of society who values others and is valued by them for what he does and not for what he obtains.[49]

Again in this local context, the role of the IBI was to provide space and opportunity for inquiry, discovery, and building confidence. The strategic and purposeful use of words and phrases like "citizen" and "free and equal member of society" projected self-determination and civic engagement as processes that not only impacted individuals but the entire community. The *Outline* demonstrated how these philosophies and values were evident in The East's structure and what they called "Our Family." In addition to Uhuru Sasa, The East ran *Black News* newspaper, The Black Experience in Sound, East Records, the African American Student Association, TAMU-Swee-Teast restaurant, the Kununuana food co-op, African Youth Village outside the city, and distribution services between the US and the Caribbean, South America, and Africa. The *Outline* introduced these material manifestations of ideology, and the authors underscored the values each embodied. For example, the food co-op was an enactment of Ujamaa (Cooperative Economics) and the African American Student Association program a site for Umoja (Unity).

"Education Is Not Neutral": Ahidiana Work/Study Center

Ahidiana Work/Study Center in New Orleans was a self-defined "Pan-Afrikan Nationalist Organization" in operation from 1973 to 1988. Ahidiana was home to an independent "alternative and affirmative" Black school for children ages three to five. Their *Ahidiana Work/Study Center Operating Principles* publication featured a prominent statement on the front cover that encapsulated this IBI's ideals: "Work for the people, Work for the race, Build for our future. Stay on the case!!"[50] One of Ahidiana's co-founders—Mtumishi St. Julien—wrote the first version of their fifteen-page *Operating Principles* document in 1973, and co-founder and poet Kalamu ya Salaam contributed to later editions. *Operating Principles* introduced the organization's purpose, methods, and technique before offering a primer on "institutions of power." The document concludes with "The Plan" and "The Commitment," sections outlining this IBI's numerous entities to demonstrate how words became action.

To introduce themselves and their work, Ahidiana stakeholders began with a statement of purpose and provided definitions for key words in the statement: "The purpose of Ahidiana is to strive for and maintain the national liberation of Afrikan-American people by working unceasingly to for the unification, liberation, and impendence of a.) Afrikan-American people, b.) all people of Afrikan descent and c.) the continent of Afrika as a whole."[51] Unification, liberation, and independence were not terms to be taken for granted, so each was given focal treatment in supporting statements. Ultimately, this introduction provided the foundation and context for Ahidiana's work in New Orleans and how it connected to a larger freedom struggle for people of African descent: "Finally, we say Afrikan-American people because our ancestors are Afrikan, therefore we are genetically and historically Afrikan, and because our most recent particular and unique history as well as our contemporary conditions and circumstances are American, therefore we are environmentally American."[52]

Distinguishing between "vital" and "strategic" educational institutions, Ahidiana asserted the need for people of African descent to establish the former ("controlled by us that define our needs"). Strategic institutions had a role to play, as well. Ahidiana defined "strategic" institutions as those "controlled by others," and acknowledged that these were also important for specific skillsets Black people might need. Educational institutions were inherently political and integral to providing both symbolic and physical representation of the Seven Principles of Blackness:

> Education is not *neutral* (i.e. void of value judgments and class or cultural interests) for education not only passes on knowledge and skills, the process of education also, and most important, shapes our attitudes and gives us values. To send our children to others gives others the power to shape our attitudes and values. . . . We need our own school capable of raising revolutionaries, leaders, and workers for our people.[53]

Similar to The East's *Outline*, Ahidiana's *Operating Principles* closed with tangible ways their institution building had adhered to the Nguzo Saba. This reverberated in co-founder Tayari Kwa Salaam's *Bulletin* essay where she provided specific examples of the Nguzo Saba in action when working with children. She noted Ahidiana "require[d]" teachers to "exemplify these values at all times":

> Our children must be allowed to watch and participate in the decision-making process. This is very important to their development because the practice of our values is not mechanical but is rather a creative process of weighing the relative merit of each and every variable under consideration . . . this calls for consciousness on our part. This demands that we always be aware of what we are doing and are requiring the children to do.[54]

Ahidiana extended an invitation for members and nonmembers to "stay ready" in the "struggle for self-defense and self-development through national liberation."[55] In addition to their school, Ahidiana promoted health and well-being through their "Steady Striders" health club. Like IPE and The East, Ahidiana had their own publishing company, Ahidiana Habari, which produced their quarterly magazine, *NKOMBO*. The *Operating Principles* document also noted their bookstore, "specializing in books about the Black Liberation Struggle." Ahidiana stakeholders wanted readers to know that whether they were official members of the organization or not, there were ways to support these entities. Their framing suggested that supporting the various branches of the organization was not to solely help Ahidiana but a commitment to Black people. A similar message could be found in the *Bulletin* about IPE: "Helping IPE is helping yourself."[56] Ahidiana's Black Community Organization was another extension of "The Commitment," with opportunities for community members to engage in a political education.

This chapter began with positioning of IPE and the *Bulletin* in the Chicago constellation, before expanding to consider how other IBIs were able to publish and contribute to a public conversation on Black Nationalism and education. In the next chapter I return to the "local"—IPE visionaries—to learn how their individual stories contribute a collective understanding of the mindsets and values of IPE visionaries and entities.

CHAPTER 2

"We Are Studying to Advance the Struggle"

IPE Visionaries Forecasting for Black Lives

Fresh from serving in the army during the Vietnam War, Jabari Mahiri (then Cleve Washington) began taking classes at the University of Illinois, Chicago. After a long period reading in isolation, Mahiri was grateful be to in literary community with other African Americans. His professor, Haki Madhubuti, then known as Don L. Lee, asked students to do more than read and explicate literature. Madhubuti wanted students to see writing, reading, and engaging literature as political education and a call to action. Mahiri and his peers were invigorated by their young professor's declaration, "We are studying to advance the struggle," and curious when Madhubuti invited students to check out the work he and other colleagues were doing nearby at the Institute of Positive Education (IPE). Mahiri recalled his time in Madhubuti's class and how it led to other opportunities:

> I took Haki's class along with a number of other people but two of us decided, "Let's go over to the South side and see what this guy is talking about in terms of the Institute of Positive Education . . ." I think we became the first student employees/workers at [IPE] that he was just setting up. Basically, [IPE] was a storefront with bookshelves and Haki was just putting books

in and pushing reading, pushing knowledge from an Afrocentric perspective and we were really hungry for that . . . my classmate and I stayed with IPE for at least fifteen, sixteen, eighteen years.[1]

One of Mahiri's first jobs at IPE was going through local newspapers and periodicals to cut out articles that could inform IPE visionaries regarding how to think about and prepare for complexities of the struggle for Black liberation pertinent to Black Chicagoans. Though IPE visionaries did not refer to themselves as futurists, the seemingly mundane task of data collection is a step toward focused imagining and planning for possible futures, which futurists refer to as forecasting. Articles and newspaper clippings provided IPE with signals: "small or local innovation or disruption [that has] . . . potential to grow in scale and geographic distribution."[2] Such signals can be helpful to "anticipate a highly uncertain future," and, in 1969, when IPE was founded, uncertainty did characterize the precariousness of Black life and Black lives in Chicago, the United States, and the world. IPE co-founders and visionaries were intentional about leveraging literary imagination to envision the future, considered Black writers to have foresight and insight, and considered writing a portal to action. As I learned more about IPE's visionaries individually, I learned how the collective was anchored to and through shared desire to imagine and create a new reality for Black people that would include access to robust education opportunities, economic independence, and—perhaps most important—self-love and communal consciousness steeped in equity and justice.

This chapter unpacks the journeys that several IPE co-founders and/or visionaries took to becoming institution builders, offering pedagogical portraits of co-founder Haki Madhubuti and others. Madhubuti also established and served as editor of IPE's literary journal, *Black Books Bulletin*, and the Black Pages pamphlet series. Prior to co-creating IPE, Madhubuti was a renowned poet, founder of Third World Press, and architect of the Black Arts Movement. Everyone I spoke with named Madhubuti as the catalyst for most IPE endeavors and their own involvement. Another co-founder, Carol D. Lee (née Easton), led IPE's school efforts, published a children's book with Third World Press, and contributed articles to *Black Books Bulletin* on education and the role of literary interpretation for young learners. Soyini Walton (née Rochelle Ricks) was another IPE co-founder and lead science educator and curriculum developer for the preschool. Walton taught in Chicago Public Schools prior to joining the IPE family and later became principal at one of IPE's charter schools and continued to contribute in myriad capacities. Kimya Moyo (née Saundra Malone) supported IPE's early efforts across programs, primarily as lead math educator and curriculum developer. A Chicago Public School teacher prior to teaching for IPE, Moyo also assisted with selling books for Third World Press like other teachers to help raise their salaries. The final IPE visionary profiled, Jabari Mahiri (né Cleve Washington), served as managing editor of *Black Books Bulletin* and supported all IPE entities. Like Walton and Moyo, Mahiri was a Chicago Public School teacher.

This is not a complete list of IPE co-founders or staff members. I started with Madhubuti, Lee, and Walton—who continue to guide IPE—and they pointed me to Moyo and Mahiri.[3] My aim is to demonstrate the varied pathways of Black institution builders and traditions from which they emerged, and, more specifically, how IPE visionaries came to understand the work of institution building as inextricably linked to the roles of Black literature and the literary imagination in/for dreaming about and building sustainable futures for Black people. Every visionary I interviewed had their children attend IPE's African-centered preschool, the New Concept Development Center, which served preschool through third grade. I refer to the individual narratives of IPE visionaries in this chapter as pedagogical portraits because I draw from oral history interviews and analysis of written material to portray what informs their worldview and influences their pedagogy, as educators.[4] While those whose stories I share assert that the power of their work lay in the collective, this chapter also highlights personal lived experiences and culminating moments that brought each of them *to* the work of forecasting and futuring for Black lives.

IPE and its visionaries also offer a unique window to examine an IBI with shared leadership. Though undeniably the catalyst for much of the institution building, Haki Madhubuti intentionally removed himself from the center of IPE operations to demonstrate one of the Seven Principles of Blackness—collective work and responsibility. Recent scholarship has been more attentive to the work of women in the Black Power and Black Arts movements countering narratives of key figures (typically male).[5] IPE attempted to imagine and enact something different: Black women and men were invited and expected to have an equal hand in supporting and educating children.

With respect to context, the Black Arts Movement was taking root nationally and internationally, when visions of and actions toward the establishment of IPE began. The Black Arts Movement is often associated with poet LeRoi Jones's transition from Greenwich Village to Harlem, after the 1965 assassination of Malcolm X. In Harlem, Jones started the Black Arts Repertory Theatre/School and became Amiri Baraka. Chicago, at that time, already had institution builders who had successfully centered the role of written, visual, and performance art. *Negro Digest* (later *Black World*), edited by Hoyt Fuller, was based in Chicago and published by Black-owned Johnson Publications. Margaret Taylor-Burroughs and Charlie Burroughs's Ebony Museum of Negro History and Art had been established in 1961, and the Organization of Black American Culture was a thriving collective of writers, poets, and activists seeking to "alter the ways African Americans in Chicago thought about art, power, and their city."[6] Madhubuti and other IPE visionaries were influenced by macro networks growing nationally and micro networks taking root in Chicago, and became emboldened by constellations of Black thought, creativity, design, and institution building taking place at the time. IPE's enduring power and ability to link past, present, and future has, perhaps, been its greatest asset, and its visionaries offer valuable insight into the role of Black institutions, as well as rationale for and practices of intentionally planning and mapping futures for future generations.

In listening to interviews with Madhubuti, one might hear him offer elements of his story in different ways, at different times, but always with the same premise: art saved him. What he has written and shared with interviewers across time and space reveals the centrality of art in Madhubuti's life and as his compass. In an exploration of jazz literature, Brent Hayes Edwards revisits an analysis of oral history wherein literary scholar Alessandro Portelli asserts that whenever oral testimonies "depart" from facts, opportunities arise to learn from people "as imagination, symbolism, and desire emerge." For example, in tracing origin stories about the naming of *The Cricket: Black Music in Evolution*, a jazz journal created by poet and Black Arts Movement architect Amiri Baraka that published Madhubuti's early work, Hayes underscores that "what is misremembered can be the source of innovation," an awareness perhaps more important than confirming "specific facts about the origin story of the journal's namesake."[7]

As a historical ethnographer, I know all too well the extent to which oral history as method comes under scrutiny for reliability, and well understood my role as "worthy witness" to the stories, innovations, and rememberings of IPE visionaries whose songs and work are unfinished. IPE visionaries continue to evolve, with respect to how they viewed and view themselves in the context of institution building.[8] Here, I explore IPE visionaries as futurists and their institution building as an act of futuring, noting that their stories capture what can happen when a collective or movement not only focuses forward but also intentionally engages in a collaborative process of imagining and enacting. Forecasting is meant to be provocative, and indeed, the boldness of imagining and pursuing a Black nation within a nation, with Black people self-reliant and economically independent, felt unimaginable to many a person.

"We Needed to Find Writers": Haki Madhubuti

"I hated myself," Haki Madhubuti stated, describing how, as little Don L. Lee, he tried throughout childhood to navigate and make sense of conditions of dire poverty under which his mother, Helen Maxine Graves Lee, had to subject herself to dehumanizing encounters just to survive.[9] Though Madhubuti has shared many aspects of his mother's story in his memoir and in interviews, there's much he's chosen not to share. "I didn't want to just shock people," he said to me of his self-restraint. Though their time together was very prematurely ended by her murder, Madhubuti credits his mother for the foundations of his lifelong journey with literature. Madhubuti recounts how his mother sent him at age fourteen or fifteen to a Detroit Public Library with instructions to check out a book called *Black Boy*, by Richard Wright. Embarrassed, teenage Don L. Lee decided he could not, would not, go to "the white library" requesting a book with that title:

> I went to the shelf, found it, put it to my chest, and walked in the people's section of the library [to] sit down and begin to read. . . . I could not take my eyes off *Black Boy*. I read over half the book before the library closed, checked the book out, ran home. Didn't give it to my mother, went to the room that my sister and I shared and started reading the book. So, I read it in twenty-four hours. Less than twenty-four hours. And gave it to my mother the next day, went back to the library and checked out everything Richard Wright had published. So that was the beginning of my being saved by art and being saved by the written word.

"Saved" was a word Madhubuti employed multiple times to describe his relationship to art, especially the literary arts, during our time together. After reading *Black Boy*, Madhubuti dug into *White Man, Listen!*, a collection of lectures Wright gave in Europe. In a chapter entitled "The Literature of the Negro in the United States," Wright reviews the writings of Alexander Pushkin, Alexander Dumas, Phillis Wheatley, and others, asserting that Negro writers had to cultivate their own voices as people with Black experiences and ways of knowing. "Our world is not their world," posits Wright, reflecting on so-called Negro writers, "we write out of what life gives us in the form of experience."[10] Contrasting Phillis Wheatley to Margaret Walker, as an example, Wright underscores that Walker's images could not have been imaginable to Wheatley.

The Black Arts Movement was incubated in the intersection of these types of divergent opportunities to imagine promising possible futures for Black people. Madhubuti would become one of those voices, leveraging his experience to create new images of Black life centering Black perspectives. Madhubuti was struck by Wright's revelations about writers who inspired him and used the book as his course of study:

> That really began my formal education in terms of Black literature . . . after I read [*White Man, Listen!*] I began to systematically read those writers and that is really what saved me because as I read those writers, I was in

music. I thought I was going to be a musician and I was halfway decent. I played the trumpet in high school band and all that stuff but between the problems happening at school and happening at home and because I had to work full time to help take care of our home, I could not pursue music.

Beyond providing context for how Madhubuti became a creator, innovator, and preserver of Black Arts and literary arts, this testimony is part of a remarkable pattern of Black institution builders having to establish pathways for grappling with anti-Blackness and their own mis-education, a popular concept from this era, to make sense of what "Black" was, is, and could be. As much as the story is about Madhubuti's entry into art and being saved by art, it is also about him as a worker and developing a distinct work ethic at a young age. The messages Madhubuti, who was born in Little Rock, Arkansas, in 1942, remembers receiving as a boy in 1940s and '50s Detroit suggested that Blackness was intertwined with skin tone and hair texture. Madhubuti's 2005 memoir, *Yellow Black*, in fact explores some of the tensions Black people with light skin experience around being viewed as "not Black enough"—an assertion Madhubuti refutes by illuminating how all Black people are engaged in struggle. It was only later in life, though, that he grew to understanding Blackness as an always nuanced convergence of color, culture, and consciousness.[11] Of course, Madhubuti was not alone in his journey, as other Black Americans were also interpolating their Blackness beyond the monolithic images of who gets counted as respectable, valuable, and worthy.

Following the murder of his mother, young Haki Madhubuti was sent to live with his father in Chicago, which was like "living with a stranger." When it became clear that this living arrangement would not be safe or sustainable, he rented a room at the YMCA, completed high school, and got "more involved with music," then more broadly "involved with other artists." Able for the first time to access a quiet environment he could largely control, Madhubuti asserted that he became "a lot more methodical" about reading the works of Black writers. This approach continued even when he enlisted in the army: "I read close to a book a day and wrote about a 250-word essay on each book." Yet, while stationed at Fort Sheridan, Illinois, he remembers feeling acutely, "there's nobody you can talk to . . . nobody who even wants to listen to this kind of stuff." His military experience also involved both isolation and abuse, intense and harmful experiences that taught Madhubuti a very valuable lesson: he didn't want to take orders from people who didn't like him ... or from people who were less intelligent than he was.

Curious about an advertisement for the Ebony Museum of Negro History and Art (later renamed Jean Baptiste Pointe DuSable Museum), which Margaret and Charles Burroughs had established in their home on Chicago's South Side, Madhubuti wondered whether this might be a community where he could be in dialogue and even debate about what he had been reading. His knock on the door of the Burroughs' home and museum launched many relationships with Black artists, intellectuals, and institution builders. Madhubuti recalls a few key things holding his attention that day he knocked. Margaret Burroughs was the first Black woman he ever saw wearing a "natural," and she was in her kitchen printmaking using a linocut process, which he had also never seen. "She looked at me and said, 'What do you want, boy?'" Still staring at her, he said something like, "I'm just kind of confused. I've been reading all this literature, there's nobody to talk to." Mrs. Burroughs sent the nineteen-year-old upstairs, where he was greeted by Charles Burroughs, who self-identified as "partially reared in the USSR" and was a fluent speaker of Russian. Charles Burroughs introduced Madhubuti to Russian and Marxist literature, which came in handy later, for "fighting Black Negro Marxists in the seventies," which he eventually did on the pages of *The Black Scholar* journal, noting that he was very critical of Black Marxists because "all they do is talk."[12]

Madhubuti wanted to do more than talk, and found new ways to excavate space for reading, writing, thinking, discussing, debating, and institution building with other artists and educators. Learning from and with the Burroughs, through whom he met Dudley Randall, the poet and publisher from Detroit who launched Broadside Press, Madhubuti was inspired to establish his own publishing company, Third World Press. Forging a collaborative relationship, Randall included young Madhubuti's work in Broadside Press offerings and they co-published projects together with Third World Press: "There's a lot of this history people just don't know, unless you were there. You can't read this stuff because very few people know about it. . . . I made a decision. This is not a choice. This is a decision. Too many of our people make choices within the parameters of other people's decisions. Third World Press was a decision. Institute of Positive Education was a decision."

The creation of IPE's school, the New Concept Development Center, was also a decision. Initially a Saturday school, IPE visionaries and the families who supported the school became clear that they needed a full-time option. Madhubuti admitted that his wife and partner, Safisha Madhubuti, would likely "contest" his recollection that creating the schools was entirely her idea. He said they were walking—something they did a lot because they couldn't afford to do anything else—and when he asked, "What do we need?" She responded, "We need schools." In his essay "The Need for Afrikan education," Madhubuti argues that Black people have "been taught to work against [themselves]" and must lead the effort to educate their own—leveraging the Seven Principles of Blacknesss, or the Nguzo Saba, with particular attention to Ujima (collective work and responsibility) and Umoja (unity).[13] Madhubuti's views on this have not waivered:

> Any people who are in control of their own cultural imperatives [must be] about the healthy replication of themselves. You cannot, in a healthy way, replicate yourself unless you're dealing with the children. This is why we started the schools. You can't be serious about liberation if you're sending your children to people who hate you or [teachers] who are there because it's their job. We have people with us because it's their mission and we found out quite early that we didn't have the books. So we said, "Okay, we need to find writers and authors and publish these books ourselves."

Education and school creation was the center piece for IBIs whose leaders sought to do more than provide Black children with academic foundations.[14] Madhubuti understood education and, more specifically, literature, as an essential tool for cultivating generations of Black people who would love themselves and value their contributions to the world, while also developing foresight to consider the needs of Black people. Here, I will state the obvious . . . futures work has its canon and most of the highly regarded futurists are white males. In fact, Madhubuti shared a story of reading Alvin Toffler's *Future Shock* and credits this book with planting in his mind the possibility that he could commute between Washington, DC, where he had been offered a teaching position at Howard University, and Chicago, where he wanted to remain firmly planted.

"We Had a Responsibility": Carol D. Lee (Safisha Madhubuti)

For the record, Carol D. Lee did refute the claim that IPE's schools were her idea. She gave credit to Haki Madhubuti, citing his "Haki vision" and ability to rally collaborators.[15] Unlike her partner, collaborator, and husband, Carol Lee was born and raised in Chicago, where she matriculated through public schools before earning her Bachelor of Arts in the teaching of secondary English in 1966. When she graduated, the Black Arts Movement was flowering with a strong presence in Chicago, quite a powerful phenomenon to behold for someone born in 1945, according to Lee: "Coming of age in '66, graduating, coming into this world where [institution building] is going on . . . I think that parallels today with the whole Black Lives Matter movement and climate change activism."

Lee's foray into teaching was through Operation Breadbasket (later Operation PUSH), where she met Hannibal Afrik, founder of Shule ya Watoto, an Independent Black Institution in Chicago.[16] Operation Breadbasket, according to Lee, had more Black teachers than the Chicago Teachers Union at the time. A young African American woman of that era was expected to be satisfied with a teaching job that provided steady income and benefits—a topic that also came up with another IPE visionary, Soyini Walton—yet Lee's continued intellectual curiosity led her to the English Department at the University of Chicago. There, her thesis examined the Black Arts Movement and, more specifically, the poetry of Don L. Lee, whom she met while conducting research for her thesis. Although she had never read any Black authors in elementary or high school, or as an undergraduate, despite her focus on the teaching of English, Carol D. Lee was sure this *would not* be the experience of children she taught. Indeed, the research agenda she would develop later during her professorial career focused on what she refers to as "cultural modeling," using African American vernacular and ways of being and knowing to engage in literary analysis and interpretation.[17] Lee's road to the Black consciousness she came to devote her life to was unpaved. According to Lee, "My mother was the most important influence on my life, but it wasn't about activism. It was about personal responsibility and internal strength." While her childhood home did not have books, there were plenty of locally published *Ebony* and *Jet* magazines.

When *Jet* published the image of an African American boy from Chicago severely mutilated and unrecognizable in his casket, Lee said this became an immediate and forever "stamp" in her memory. Emmett Till's story rang close to home for many Black Chicagoans, as his gruesome murder occurred during a visit with relatives in Mississippi, a familiar journey for African Americans in the urban North, Midwest, and West whose families had been part of the Great Migration from Southern states. At just fourteen years old, Till was accused of flirting with a white woman in August of 1955, and that woman's husband and brother-in-law went to the homes of Till's relatives, demanding the boy come with them. He was brutally tortured, beaten, and murdered. His mother, Mamie Elizabeth Till-Mobley, made the seemingly unthinkable decision to have an open-casket funeral so the world could witness white America's enduring racial terror on Black people. In the September 15, 1955, issue, *Jet* published photos, which reminded young Carol D. Lee that she already "knew where the boundaries were." Even within Chicago, she would never, as a Black child, venture downtown or into other white ethnic communities. "The implication of this story is . . . what the historical moment makes available to you," explained Lee.

Long before the murder of Emmett Till, Chicago experienced the Red Summer Riots of 1919. Eugene Williams, an African American child, was murdered at Lake Michigan Beach. When Williams's raft drifted "across the imaginary line" into an area that white patrons believed they owned, he was stoned and eventually drowned.[18] This set off a series of violent confrontations between Black and white Chicagoans that made their way off the beach. According to Jakobi Williams, the Red Summer "transformed Black Chicago residents from victims to a people who relied on their agency to defend themselves and their community from white violence."[19] However, for Lee as a young African American girl growing up in Chicago in the 1950s, the threat of white violence when one ventured outside clearly perceived boundaries continued to persist.

Another key element of Lee's story was her mother's laser-sharp focus on economic security, which, according to Lee, "was absolutely central on [my mother's] mind." Growing up in the Great Depression and losing her own mother at age sixteen, Lee's mother wanted her daughter to maintain a reliable teaching job. "So, no, it wasn't a matter of my mother saying 'Go out there. Work for Black people. Be liberated,'" Lee recalled. In fact, Lee's mother was certain her daughter had "lost" her mind when she cut her hair to wear a natural style that was a symbol of the Black Power and Black Arts movements and underscored that Black—natural and untainted with products designed to alter one's physical person—was "beautiful." Her mother became even more fretful when Lee quit her job in the Chicago City College system to launch the Institute of Positive Education, open schools, and design a curriculum with the liberation of Black people as her focus. "My mother went to her minister and asked him if he knew a psychiatrist because this man has put the hoodoo on my child," remembered Lee with a smile. "This man" was Haki Madhubuti, who would not only become Lee's partner in institution building and family building, but also a son to her mother. With other visionary movement builders, they partnered to form what Lee refers to as a "commitment to the collective" in Chicago. Lee, who later took the name Safisha Madhubuti, chose to commit to the collective by investing her time and talents in supporting children to find their gifts and creating opportunities for those gifts to reach their highest potential. Lee cited the Kemetic principles of Maat, when describing how her work was grounded in the ideal that everyone is born with perfectibility:[20]

> And I will say that across the years of working in building these institutions, one of the things that has been revelatory that took me a while [to understand] is that those of us who know the history of—let's say Harriet Tubman and Frederick Douglass—often hear these were extraordinary people. And I would say, "No, they weren't." They were ordinary human beings who understood [the] heart . . . who understood the goals that they had for themselves and for our people, and there was no barrier that was going to keep them from moving forward in that direction.

The idea that ordinary everyday people can facilitate change, imagine more equitable futures, and be of service to their people was generative. This mindset invited people to the IPE table, rather than situate visionary ideas and related work as emerging from or through one key figure. Ordinary people defined both the Black Power and the Black Arts Movements, and Chicago in the 1960s and 1970s was at the center of this building, creating, dreaming, and doing. Studying and leveraging Black writers and the Black experience as interpreted in literature was central to this work, according to Lee:

> I call on great authors. Those who stand the test of time as having the gift of second sight like priests or priestesses . . . they have insights into the conundrums of what it means to be human that they interrogate through the narratives they create. And they deal with complexities in ways that I am not sure you can do in any other way than through narrative whether it's a written literary text or visual in terms of a painting or a digital movie or whatever.

Calling on great authors was a foundational IPE value, and one can see the imprint of literature and the power of literary arts throughout the pedagogical portraits. Every visionary I interviewed cited books and how their institution-building efforts and the work of Black authors were intertwined. Lee often cited Toni Morrison and her novel *Beloved* as her first encounter of feeling, viscerally, the pangs of enslavement, as Sethe grapples with the decision to take the life of her baby rather than surrender the baby to her former enslavers, who considered her baby their property. She also referenced Ayi Kwei Armah's *Two Thousand Seasons*, which begins with "We are not a people of yesterday . . ." to launch a harrowing story of enslavement while also nodding to the legacy of hope, endurance, and redefinition often tethered to the Black experience through/out literature. Lee understood these texts and others as tools to support institution builders grappling with the complexities and conundrums of life as a collective of Black people building for Black people. Her use of "second sight" is not a reference to clairvoyance as much as a practical tool to anticipate challenges and imagine the other side of the challenges. Lee was adamant that to understand IPE was to also understand the vision for their science and mathematics

FIGURE 2.1. Institute of Positive Education planning meeting at their first "storefront" on the South Side of Chicago. Carol D. Lee (Safisha Madhubuti) is seated on the right side of the table, Haki Madhubuti (Don L. Lee) sits next to her, and Jabari Mahiri (Cleve Washington) is leaning against the boxes behind Madhubuti. Reprinted with permission from K. Kofi Moyo.

curriculum, led by Soyini Walton and Kimya Moyo respectively, women who, like Lee, understood academic disciplines to be interconnected and part of a continuum.

"We Had to Be Self-Critical": Soyini Walton

When Soyini Walton met Don L. Lee in June 1968, she admitted that their first encounter "transformed" her and that Lee "left a big impression."[21] The specific date resides in Walton's memory because "I went home that night and washed out my press and curl and I've been natural ever since." What inspired her the most about their meeting was that, in addition to having published his own work, Lee had a mission for other Black people to do the same. "His idea," began Walton, "was to first publish ourselves, our voices, books, magazines, poems, by and about Black people. He said we needed to educate ourselves. We could not continue to just take chances on sending our children to other people to be educated . . . we needed to control that." While Don L. Lee had an immediate impact on Ms. Walton, he was not the first person to encourage her to "think Black"—the namesake of one of Lee's early publications. "My radicalization was smoldering . . . Don L. Lee brought it more into a full fire. But it was smoldering because of my father. My father was a great intellect and avid reader. He really taught me how the world works." Second-generation Chicagoans, Walton's grandparents had migrated from Mississippi. Her father was a community activist and a "race man," with "leanings toward socialism." Elements of Black Nationalism and challenging racism and capitalism were thus part and parcel of Walton's life experiences. She was already teaching in Chicago Public Schools before being recruited to IPE in 1966:

> I started teaching fourth grade in the city's Englewood neighborhood. We were known to be a really rough neighborhood and so forth. But the community was established and a lot of people had their own homes and the families were appreciative of a good teacher and a good education. I was radicalized when I started teaching. . . . I removed the American flag from my classroom and I had the children so pumped up about why we shouldn't have an American flag . . . I made up my own pledge. I probably have it written down somewhere.

Building on her already "smoldering" radicalization, Walton refers to her time with IPE as coming into "full fire." The fire aesthetic was a popular theme in Black Arts Movement poetry and writing. LeRoi Jones and Larry Neal's 1968 anthology of Afro American writing was aptly named *Black Fire*. Later, Sonia Sanchez would rekindle the metaphor in a poem/keynote address entitled "Catch the Fire."[22] Like other Black teachers in public school systems during this period, Walton found few opportunities to work collectively and even fewer spaces to express one's Blackness. Her story as a teacher, for example, mirrors institution-builder Jitu Weusi's experiences in New York Public Schools. In her examination of Black politics and education reform in Chicago, Elizabeth Todd-Breland opens a chapter on IBIs with Walton's story, noting that Walton worked at IPE "before and after work and on the weekends" and "donated half of her pay" from her public school teaching.[23] Todd-Breland underscores how Walton's teaching experience at IPE was unique, given that most Black teachers in Chicago at that era remained in the public system, where they would "simultaneously fight for improvements in schools serving Black students and for recognition, representation, and a greater voice in the teaching force and teacher's union."[24]

In addition to co-founding and working at IPE, Walton became the science curriculum design lead and also director of IPE's preschool, the New Concept Development Center. Just as Walton's activism can be traced to her father, her interest in and passion for science began in early childhood. Walton's parents encouraged her to explore and "made space" for her to read, draw, play, and investigate. "I remember finding a dead bird," Walton recalled, "When you're a child, you don't have all those inhibitions." A young Walton began experimenting with her discovery. Despite interest in science, she did feel "directed and funneled into female occupations," and recalled being told by high school educators to take secretarial courses focused on stenography and transcription. After high school, Walton attended Chicago State University (then called Chicago Teachers College). "I got a degree in education but I really wanted to major in teaching science, so I took all the science courses that are real." Following the footsteps of her mother, who returned to school later in life, Walton returned for additional degrees in science and fulfilled her vision of becoming a working engineer before returning to IPE in a different capacity—lead of the institution's charter school.

Walton was always intentional about linking science to other disciplines, beginning with her work at IPE's New Concept Development Center, where the preschool science curriculum she designed mirrored her own childhood curiosity and freedom to explore. She recalled IPE being across from a "nice, juicy vacant lot" on 76th Street and Cottage that she and her students used as their laboratory: "A social science question we had was, 'What does it mean that this lot is vacant in our community?' And, then there was a log with all kinds of insects. We would come back and write about the vacant lot, so that includes Language Arts. We see science as art and art in science. We see music in science and science is music. Math is music . . . it's a worldview."

This world view and seeing the disciplines as a continuum, as opposed to separate and distinct units taught in isolation, guided IPE's work. *Black Books Bulletin*, for example, modeled this continuum of vast interests in issues dedicated to "Science and Struggle," "Education," "Black Psychology," and others. Walton recognized that the *Bulletin* was ahead of its time and that IPE's work in Chicago needed other books and publications where visionaries could reflect on the terms and concepts of the day—Black Nationalism, Black Cultural Nationalism, Pan-Africanism, Marxism, Neo-Marxism, and the like—and engage with other thinkers:

> [*Black Books Bulletin*] was critical and forward thinking because while we are embracing everything African and everything Black, we knew we had to be self-critical. So it was important for us to have that literary bulletin so that we could critique things that were being written. We had to think deeply. And when you think deeply and make decisions about the direction of the organization . . . you're going to advise the community what to do as well.

FIGURE 2.2. Far Left: Soyini Walton talking to members of the IPE community, including Jabari Mahiri and Carol D. Lee, during a Kwanza event. Reprinted with permission from K. Kofi Moyo.

The Black community would be looking to IPE, and IPE needed to be self-aware and self-critical as it positioned itself among the larger landscape of Black Cultural Nationalism, as initiated by Malauna Karenga and expanded by Amiri Baraka, as well as Pan-Africanism, as articulated by Marcus Mosiah Garvey and others. IPE and its visionaries did not blindly follow any one ideology but sought to understand the needs of Black people in Chicago first. The *Bulletin* sought to go beyond offering more definitions to synthesize what could be utilized for the now, and the future, of and by Black people. IPE used the *Bulletin* to provide concrete and specific tools—not only books but also who (authors, publishers), what (ideas, concepts, critiques, and analysis of various authors and thinkers), and where (locations of Black publishers throughout the world).

"We Were Developing a New Way of Life": Dr. Kimya Moyo

Kimya Moyo (Saundra Malone) experienced a different journey to Chicago, than did Madhubuti, Lee, or Walton. Born and raised in Cincinnati, Ohio, Moyo moved to Illinois to attend Northwestern University. It was 1965:

> There were three Black girls on campus . . . a senior from Birmingham, Alabama, a sophomore from Winston-Salem, North Carolina, and myself. And I remember on that first day when my mother and father dropped me off at my dorm and these white girls said they weren't going to live with me. So I didn't have a roommate for some time . . . that was my first introduction [and I thought], "What is this? And why am I at this school?"

Moyo's parents, and her father in particular, hoped she would join the family business after graduation. He was into real estate, owned apartment buildings and land, and imagined his only child getting into insurance or a field that could expand the family business in new directions. "I just gravitated toward teaching," Moyo recalled, sharing stories of time with children in her neighborhood and always wanting to play "teacher." Despite her father carrying a different vision, Moyo explained that her parents "thankfully . . . didn't make me do anything." This liberated her to pursue her passion for teaching. About the first, very challenging days she experienced at Northwestern, Moyo spoke of feeling isolated and searching for any semblances of "home," in this unfamiliar place. "Home" was a word Moyo returned to throughout her interview, as she described how patterns of experience at Northwestern fueled her strong motivation and desire to find and sustain community.

Early on, "looking for Black folks," Moyo went for a walk and encountered a small group of young African American men—student athletes. "They were happy to see me, and I was happy to see them!" Moyo exclaimed. They brought her to a house where a man named Doc provided a "home away from home" for African American student athletes. Doc in fact worked at Northwestern and extended the invitation to all African American students. "So that house became my house for four years," Moyo recounted, "Those people became my family for four years and I was there every weekend." By junior year, she and several African American students had concluded, "They didn't really want us up here. They weren't preparing for us." The "they"? University staff. The "us"? African American students. Moyo and more than one hundred peers planned a sit-in at the administration building.

So, we took over the administration building. And that bound us together. That opened my eyes to a lot of things. Just the whole taking over of the building itself was my first activist act, so to speak. . . . The night before the sit-in, I called my parents. I couldn't tell them what was going on because we knew our phones were bugged. . . . That next morning, when my father was on his way to work in Cincinnati, he was in the car and heard on the news that Black students at Northwestern had taken over the building. So Daddy just bypassed his exit to get to work and went straight to the airport to come to Northwestern and get me out of the building. So maybe my first activist act was to say, "No, Daddy, I'm staying in the building. You go over to Doc's house . . . I'll be okay."

The 1968 "Bursar's office takeover" at Northwestern yielded several developments in the areas of curriculum, housing, and financial aid, and is known in university history as the "May 4th Agreement."[25] Another important outcome from the "takeover" intersected with Moyo's future work at IPE when Lerone Bennett Jr. was hired as a visiting professor in a department that came to be African American studies.[26] Bennett—former editor of *Ebony* magazine—Moyo's first African American history professor at Northwestern, was hired as a direct result of the Bursar's office takeover and had been anointed by the Black community as "our kind of historian" because he used the lens of journalism to make African American history accessible and available to people beyond "academics." Little did Moyo know then that she would reconnect with his ideas and work in her role at IPE.

After graduation, Moyo moved to Chicago and taught math on the West Side at a school down the street from where Black Panther Fred Hampton was murdered by police while sleeping next to his pregnant fiancé. When we spoke, she recalled being "right there in the midst of everything"—and feeling dissatisfied and unfulfilled as a Chicago Public School teacher. It was a fellow teacher who suggested that Moyo connect with a local drama group, Kuumba Theatre, as a creative outlet, noting that the group not only staged local plays but also traveled further afield with an ensemble. It was Kuumba Theater's creator, Val Gray Ward, who suggested that Moyo visit the IPE to learn about their plans to launch a school. "It was not even two years before I quit the public school," Moyo remembered. Between her drama group and IPE, she described finding "home" in Chicago and several things that still stand out about that time in her life. When she came on board at IPE, Madhubuti told Moyo she had to "raise" her own salary, which all IPE teachers did, either by selling Third World Press books or working with IPE's typesetting company. Moyo and her IPE co-visionaries were in their twenties. "We were just kids . . . we dared to do stuff and did it!" Moyo exclaimed. "Our parents thought we were crazy, sure enough. But that was where we were at that time in our lives. I wouldn't trade it for anything."

Mathematics was Moyo's other "home." In Chicago Public Schools, Moyo taught high school mathematics. Her pedagogy transformed as she worked with much younger children at IPE's New Concept Development Center:

> I think I became more intentional about teaching math from a utilitarian or African-centered perspective. . . . I found that whatever it is that

you're teaching has to be relevant. What are the origins of mathematics? Why are we doing this? How does it facilitate anything we do? And once I started doing that, I recognized that teaching math is no different than teaching whatever other discipline it is that you're teaching. It is about how you relate to kids.

Relationships, according to Moyo, were the foundation of her teaching. In fact, she talked about her 5-Rs of teaching mathematics: relationships, recitation, repetition, ritual, and routine. Ultimately, Moyo believes the work at IPE overall was teaching and learning and doing from an African-centered perspective, "expanding the lens" of Black children, and creating a culture of collaborative thinking and idea generation.

"We Were Reading in Concert": Jabari Mahiri

Distinct words or phrases can be pulled out as crucial distillations of IPE visionaries' journeys of becoming institution builders. I've mentioned Haki Madhubuti's as "saved." Carol D. Lee's could be "the historical moment." For Soyini Walton, nods to fire, and for Moyo, "home." For Jabari Mahiri (Cleve Washington), managing editor of *Black Books Bulletin* and officiant of Haki and Carol's marriage ceremony, I would likely employ "hungry."

Like Lee, Mahiri was born in Chicago, two years later. His parents were part of the Great Migration who, despite having received minimal formal schooling themselves, were able to provide for their children and buy a modest home in Chicago, near well-resourced schools. "When I look back on it now, [what my parents did] was magic," exclaimed Mahiri when recounting his childhood. Despite being exposed to an excellent education, Mahiri said he initially had no plans to attend college. He got a good factory job making $2.25 an hour and eventually was drafted into the Army. While serving in Vietnam for eighteen months, Mahiri asserts that he "became political" because, like Haki Madhubuti, he "had a lot of time to read."

Having read works such as *The Autobiography of Malcolm X* and *The Man Who Cried I Am*, Mahiri left the army "hungry" for African American literature and places to discuss that literature. When he returned to college, he enrolled in Madhubuti's African American literature class and was among the students recruited to work at the Institute of Positive Education, ultimately serving as managing editor of *Black Books Bulletin*. "We were being nourished by these amazing thinkers and activists like Lerone Bennett Jr., who was pushing *Before the Mayflower*."

My own ethnographic research has made clear the pattern that participatory literacy communities in Black America often blur speaker-audience boundaries. I have experienced and explored this phenomenon, for example, in Black-owned and -operated bookstores and "open mic" events.[27] In a similar vein, Madhubuti designed his African American literature class to prepare students to engage in large-scale collaborative projects and build community through the literary arts. And, according to Mahiri, this preparation combined reading, critiquing, writing, and exchanging ideas:

> We were part of a larger cultural complex when we were sitting in class. It was certainly what Don L. Lee was doing in terms of bringing us together . . . and it was a traditional lecture format but it was the kind of texts he was bringing. . . . We were reading in concert with each other and that was food to our souls because we had not experienced anything like that . . . we felt like we were part of a national movement . . . and, here, these texts—literary texts and historical texts—were giving us insights. . . . It was like we were just hungry for the nutrition that these texts were offering us that we'd never had before.

Mahiri continued with the metaphor of nutrition, using "nourished" to describe the feeling of interacting with thinkers and activists and being able to distinguish between "fresh fruits and vegetables" or this new way of engaging with literature and institution building, as opposed to "what is in these cans." Author Michael Datcher used a similar metaphor when describing his experiences sharing his writing in Black bookstores, which he referred to as "soul food" and a stark contrast to other bookstores.[28]

Mahiri was involved in every IPE entity, though he feels it was as managing editor of *Black Books Bulletin* for a decade that he and IPE most tangibly contributed to the work of imagining specific, practical, ambitious, and hopeful Black futures. Mahiri noted that the Nation of Islam had a presence on the South Side and the Communiversity was inspiring many Black Chicagoans. "It's like coming full circle with another generation," explained Mahiri, "It is futuristic because now we're in a position where we can reflect back and ask, 'How did all of this come to be?' and to consider how was our work influenced by the work of others."

Collective Process, Collaborative Power

While every IPE visionary has an incredibly compelling background and story, none of those with whom I conducted interviews were interested in being celebrated as individuals. Haki Madhubuti gave credit to his wife, Carol D. Lee, for the idea to start their school, which she adamantly denied and asserted was all his idea. Jabari Mahiri talked about Haki Madhubuti's brilliance in creating *Black Books Bulletin* and referred to Lee as "the brains" of the school. Lee shifted my gaze to Kimya Moyo and Soyini Walton when we spoke, underscoring their critical input regarding design of the math and science curricula, respectively. Mahiri's role as managing editor was, in fact, key to the leadership and success of *Black Books Bulletin*.

Mahiri, who was serving as the faculty director of the Leadership Programs at the University of California, Berkeley, at the time of our interview, thought a lot about the leadership structure of IPE. He described a distributed leadership model and people working side by side—some being paid, others volunteering. While studies of the Black Power and Black Arts Movement have often focused on sexism and gender inequality, Mahiri articulated IPE's view that men ought and were "expected to have an equal role in the education of their children": "We had high involvement with the kids as men in the organization, as well as the women. We didn't have an equal number of men and women teaching in the school but there was certainly an emphasis on men taking up nurturing relationship with young people."

As was the case with the children of other IPE visionaries, all three of Mahiri's sons attended IPE's New Concept Development Center, through third grade. This offered a work-life balance that remains enviable to many of us in the workplaces of today. It also offered constant opportunities of/for intergenerational dynamics and engagement and values

62 · FUTURING BLACK LIVES

affirmation. "Everything we do has a repercussion," offered Moyo, "It's like the waves, the ripples in the water. They are going to affect generations and generations and generations behind us. And if we don't have that vision to understand and know that, then there's something not right with how we see the role that we play today." In Mahiri's words, "There were always these bridges being crossed." And one of IPE's most clear and powerful approaches to bridgebuilding and idea crosswalks was, without a doubt, *Black Books Bulletin*, the literary journal IPE published quarterly from 1971 to 1981. To give this truth the same level of attention placed on it by the IPE co-founders and visionaries I had the opportunity to interview, I will now turn to how that literary tool both embodied dialogue between the Black Power and Black Arts movements and also articulated and demonstrated the role of the literary arts in imagining and pursuing Black freedom.

CHAPTER 3

Between "Precariousness" and "Possibility"

The Emergence of *Black Books Bulletin*

In the summer of 1976, the *Black Books Bulletin* (the *Bulletin*) editorial team published a themed issue titled "Black People and the Future." To reflect and amplify this theme, Institute of Positive Education (IPE) co-founder and editor of the *Bulletin* Haki Madhubuti commissioned local Chicago artist and gallery owner Yaoundé Olu to create the cover. Olu translated Madhubuti's vision as an opportunity to create an image of Black people "not limited to a particular way of being." Against a deep black canvas, two figures, one male and one female, in "transmitter helmets"—for the purposes of "communication and navigation"—were adorned with cosmic patterns on their faces, punctuated with a "stylized atom" on their chins. These "melanated people" from the future embodied what Madhubuti and other Black Arts Movement visionaries and institution builders of that era wanted: Black people "to be their own light" and "bring light" where "darkness" existed.[1]

Published by IPE in Chicago, the *Bulletin* was a literary journal that described itself as "the most comprehensive reviewing medium for books by and about black people," with a simultaneous commitment to publishing "the newest writings by some of our most gifted minds." While Olu's cover art depicting technologically and spiritually advanced Black

63

explorers may have appeared futuristic and out-of-reach in 1976, the feature interview with Maulana Karenga not only anchored this issue with the pragmatism of IPE visionaries who shared unrelenting future-oriented focus on Black self-determination, but also represented IPE's desire to ensure that art was accessible and functional.

The black and white image taken by K. Kofi Moyo of IPE's Baraza ya Kazi, discussed in this book's introduction, may seem a great contrast to this futuristic cover painted by Olu. The tools with which her mela-nated subjects were equipped—transmitter helmets and a space travel machine—offered windows into imagined futures. Moyo's subjects in the black and white photo, on the other hand, offered a true glimpse into IPE's futuring *process* for networks of Black artists, educators, par-ents, and, in fact, everyone committed to self-determined futures for Black people. Ultimately, though, the artistic rendering of an imagined future and the photo capturing the actual work of real people futuring both signaled "a warm time of building," "a time of hope," and "a time of unlimited possibilities."[2]

This chapter examines how IPE leveraged one of its primary futuring tools, the *Bulletin* literary journal, to inform and influence Black peo-ple while providing positive images of Black life, lives, and possibilities. Encouraging engagement with texts across genres, the *Bulletin* invited its readers to consider a range of worldbuilding endeavors, in response to signals emerging from the sociopolitical context of the 1970s. A nod to physical bulletin boards displaying an array of information and activ-ity, the *Bulletin* addressed issues impacting African-descended people "wherever they may be" and cultivated Black ideas to plan for and sus-tain healthy and liberated lives.

Engaging with "significant urban trends" and their "probable impact on the future of Black people," the *Bulletin* chose Malauna Karenga to interview for the 1976 future-oriented thematic issue.[3] As a principal architect of Black Cultural Nationalism, Karenga created the Nguzo Saba (Seven Principles of Blackness, now widely known as the Seven Days of Kwanzaa) that IPE adhered to in their work and championed as a path toward Black freedom and futures. How else could Black peo-ple imagine desired futures, but by first defining Black values and culti-vating identity, purpose, and direction? Karenga's Nguzo Saba—Unity,

FIGURE 3.1. *Black Books Bulletin*'s Summer 1976 issue, "Black People and the Future." Reprinted with permission from Third World Press Foundation.

Self-Determination, Collective Work & Responsibility, Cooperative Economics, Creativity, Purpose, and Faith—provided Black people with links to their past, grounded their present, and created opportunities for them to imagine thriving collective futures. IPE did not romanticize this work, nor did Karenga. He approached the topic of Black futures by first addressing the economic, political, and cultural struggles of Black and other "Third World peoples" globally. He paused to note that his effort to contextualize these struggles was not meant to "provoke pessimism," but to project an outlook that was, in fact, quite optimistic: "Crisis is not a condition for fear and fatalism, but for audaciousness and initiative. Crisis is a time of danger and critical decision and joined with its great risks are the possibilities of great rewards. Precariousness and possibility travel together on the road to revolution, to great and profound social change. That is why critical and audacious *alternative* thought is so vital."[4]

IPE's literary journal itself embraced the intersection of precariousness and possibility, demonstrating a commitment to "critical and audacious *alternative* thought," which Karenga argued was vital to imagining Black futures. The *Bulletin*, with a circulation of 3,500, was both a compass and a map that invited readers to engage with new directions of thought, navigate Black ideas, and learn with and from scholars and practitioners. IPE positioned the journal to function as praxis and embodiment of Madhubuti's vision for transitioning from a "plan" to a "planet"—wherein Black thought, ideas, creativity, and action could be discussed, debated, and improved through literary exploration. I consider the *Bulletin* to be one of IPE's primary futuring tools, leveraging literary imagination to promote Black Cultural Nationalism, Pan-Africanism, and Black self-determination, while providing temporality to IPE's efforts to demonstrate a past (Identity), present (Purpose), and future (Direction) continuum. To this end, the *Bulletin* served as a portal between histories and futures, anchoring readers in the sociopolitical landscape of the 1970s, identifying the potential obstacles of the immediate present and near future, and envisioning pathways to Black self-determination.

In this chapter, I discuss the *Bulletin* as part of a constellation of Black publications in and beyond Chicago. I then narrow the focus to the cartography of the *Bulletin* and how the journal built on and expanded the work of IPE to create a map for Black institution building during the Black Arts Movement. I turn to a consistent section of the *Bulletin*, BBB Interviews, which featured conversations between the editorial team and Black thinkers, to demonstrate one specific pathway forward that the *Bulletin* offered people of African descent. Finally, I consider some key themes of the journal, including attention to health and wellness in Black families and communities, and how wellness can play a role in nation building.

IPE, the *Bulletin*, and Black Literate Lives

In previous work examining Black literate lives, I discussed the Black liberation movement of the 1960s and '70s as a "literacy-based movement," phrasing borrowed from institution builder Jitu Weusi (Les Campbell). Independent Black institutions and Black organizations were self-publishing books, pamphlets, newspapers, magazines, and journals, and some offered typesetting services to generate additional income. Writing, reading, speaking, and "doing" operated as a continuum worthy of being shared but also compelling enough to galvanize and nurture movement work.[5] With its first issue of the *Bulletin*, IPE became part of a national and international conversation examining Black life/lives through the lens of Blackness and the various perspectives of Black people. Long the subject of white analysis and research, the Black experience was reclaimed by Black thinkers by/through independent publishing. Friends and colleagues Dudley Randall and Hoyt Fuller particularly inspired Madhubuti's foray into publishing. Using his income as a librarian, Randall had launched Broadside Press in 1965 in Detroit, where he co-published the first edition of Madhubuti's *From Plan to Planet*. Fuller was not only the editor and the visionary behind the aforementioned *Negro Digest / Black World* (1942–1951/1961–1976), but he also spearheaded additional forms of literary activism in and beyond Chicago. More radical than *Ebony* and *Jet* magazines, *Black World* featured poets and writers from throughout the African diaspora. All three magazines were published by Johnson Publishing Company in Chicago (*Ebony* established in 1945 and *Jet* in 1951), where Black print culture had a long legacy of Black-owned, Black-operated publications (see Chapter 1). Chicago was also the site of two Nation of Islam newspapers, *Muhammad Speaks* (1960–1975) and *The Final Call* (established in 1979 by Minister Louis Farrakhan in his South Chicago home) that focused on Black life and the Black experience in Chicago.

The *Bulletin* could be in relevant conversation with research journals, newspapers, and publications that were decidedly more literary and arts focused—in whatever region they were created. Three years prior to IPE publishing the *Bulletin*, in 1969 Robert Chrisman and Nathan Hare established *The Black Scholar* in San Francisco, with a focus on Black studies and research. The San Francisco Bay Area was also home to the *Journal of Black Poetry* (1966–1973), founded by Joe Goncalves, which featured the work of Haki Madhubuti when he was still Don L. Lee, in the summer of 1968. Goncalves also started *Soulbook: The Quarterly Journal of Revolutionary AfroAmerica* (1964–1967). New York was home to *Umbra* literary journal, established in 1963 by the Society of Umbra. Tom Dent and Kalamu ya Salaam (né Val Ferdinand) established *NKOMBO*, a quarterly literary journal, in New Orleans through BLACKARTSOUTH. Printed from 1968 to 1974, *NKOMBO* was initially published as *Echoes from the Gumbo* before Dent and Salaam changed the name to reflect the origins of the word *gumbo*. Another periodical out of New Orleans, *The Black Collegian*, was launched in 1970 and gained traction among African American college students by announcing careers, internships, and information about graduate and professional schools.[6] Independent Black institutions The East in Brooklyn and the Committee for a Unified NewArk in New Jersey published the *Black News* and *Unity & Struggle* newspapers, respectively.[7] Jabari Mahiri, who became the *Bulletin*'s managing editor later in its first volume, saw the journal as making unique contributions to the body of Black print culture of the day: "[Madhubuti's] vision was beautiful because you had *The Black Scholar*, you had *The Black Collegian*, you had the *Negro Digest* being published by Johnson Publications, but nothing was happening in terms of like a focus on black children themselves. And so *Black Books Bulletin* was a literary publication, first and foremost, but it [engaged with] everything . . . education and politics, history."[8] Mahiri underscored that the *Bulletin* was "intricately linked" to IPE, a landing place for all of IPE's various tentacles. IPE visionary Kimya Moyo also talked about how all IPE entities came together with the *Bulletin*. For example, IPE held Nation Studies classes and the course reading list included Chancellor Williams's *The Destruction of Black Civilization: Great Issues of Race from 4500 BC to 2000 AD* (1971), published by Third World Press. According to Moyo, one could expect to be reading Williams's book in class and then "turn around and here comes Chancellor Williams walking down the street to IPE. . . . So, these authors and writers, and poets and everything . . . they were always in and out of our spaces."[9] In addition to Mahiri's observation that the *Bulletin* was unique in its profound interest in children and their futures, Moyo offered an image of the *Bulletin* as the visual representation of the continuum IPE sought to create between nation building and the literary arts.

IPE's commitment to educating the entire community through Nation Studies classes had a profound impact on the visionaries themselves, as they gained exposure to new ideas and ways of working for Black freedom. Mahiri recounted the synergy between Third World Press authors,

IPE guest speakers, the *Bulletin*'s featured writers and interviewees, and how the journal came to life through Nation Studies classes:

> We felt it was important to be involved in the education of the entire community and not just the children. . . . We would have speakers coming every week on a Tuesday night. We would have them at an organization's headquarters or the local library. Amazing speakers . . . and community folks . . . who can stand toe to toe with any of these scholars. This is where I first heard the term "historiography" because these guys were like "Well, you have to have the understanding of the structures of how histories are narrated and made into arguments, as well as the philosophical considerations that underpin it."[10]

Mahiri's recollection of public forums hosted by IPE highlighted a striking characteristic: featured poets, authors, and speakers were not elevated over the so-called audience. Attendees were well-read and well-prepared for discussions and debates, reinforcing Weusi's assertion that the pursuit of Black liberation was tethered to being literate and literary.[11] Indeed, as managing editor of the *Bulletin*, Mahiri immersed himself in learning from and with the authors whose work his team and community reviewed, revered, and critiqued:

> Gwendolyn Brooks was like our patron saint. She was right there in Chicago and she was always leveraging our ability to connect with other people . . . we had interactions and conversations with Toni Morrison and Wole Soyinka . . . Ayi Kwei Armah's *Two Thousand Seasons* was a really important book. But many of us took his second book even more at hand, called *The Healers*. . . . We were jointly influenced by some of the best African scholars . . . [Chinweizu's] *The West and the Rest of Us*. Chinweizu was a physicist. . . . [Harold Cruse's] *The Crisis of the Negro Intellectual* was a major book for us. And, of course, the Black writers of that time . . . Richard Wright . . . Ralph Ellison . . . obviously James Baldwin.[12]

Much has been written about Gwendolyn Brooks's journey from "Negro poet" to "Black poet," as well as her finding identity, purpose, and direction through the poet institution builders of the Black Arts

70 · FUTURING BLACK LIVES

Movement. A Pulitzer Prize–winner, Brooks enjoyed a consistent publishing career with mainstream publishers but later chose to move her poetry catalog to Third World Press. Madhubuti has documented Brooks's role as his "spiritual mother," and she played a vital role in the lives of IPE visionaries. The *Bulletin* and IPE were grounded in poetry and the arts, and Mahiri's observations show the fluid engagement of and between African and African American writers and scholars: "Our writers were mainly poets of our generation. It was Sonia Sanchez, Mari Evans, and Sterling Plumpp . . . the OBAC writer's workshop . . . so there were all of these organizations operating interconnectedly and simultaneously that were reinforcing . . . you had the writers' group . . . the artistic group doing the drama . . . the Association for the Advancement of Creative Musicians."[13]

Interviews with IPE visionaries often revealed reading lists. Mahiri was an English teacher in Chicago Public Schools and Lee taught in the Chicago City College system. Both were contributors to the *Bulletin* and authors of children's books for Third World Press. Sterling Plumpp, the *Bulletin*'s managing editor before Mahiri, was a poet whose work appeared in *Negro Digest / Black World*. Like Madhubuti and Mahiri, Plumpp had served in the US Army, and, like other IPE visionaries, he not only worked on the *Bulletin* but was deeply engaged in numerous IPE entities and published his book *Black Rituals* with Third World Press. Mahiri asserts that ultimately their work at IPE, the *Bulletin*, their schools, and the local community was inspired and driven by the force of the poets and poetry of their time. Among these were Sonia Sanchez and Mari Evans, both of whom published children's books with Third World Press and whose work was reviewed and included in the *Bulletin*'s bibliographies.

"You Are Why We Exist": Cartography of the *Bulletin*

Four years after establishing Third World Press and two years after co-founding IPE, Madhubuti and an editorial team of IPE visionaries, teachers, and collaborators published the first issue of the *Bulletin* literary journal, in 1971. Madhubuti wanted the *Bulletin* to function as a conduit between Black poets, writers, thinkers, publishers, parents, educators, and everyday people. Consistent with IPE culture, the *Bulletin* was an all-hands-on-deck endeavor. IPE teachers raised their own salaries by typesetting for the journal through IPE's typesetting company, Hieroglyphics Ink, and by selling subscriptions to the journal. IPE teachers and visionaries doubled as book reviewers and essay contributors. Since many of their children attended IPE's African-centered preschool, it was not unusual to see their children's images on the pages of the journal.

When the *Bulletin* debuted in 1971, the journal cost $2.00 an issue or $8.00 for an annual subscription. "Charter subscribers" were offered a special rate of $7.00 per year, and the inaugural issue contained a "charter subscription certificate," with a further reduction in the initial cost for the roughly sixty-page journal, which had thoughtfully designed covers and innovative layouts. Initially funded by a grant from IPE, Madhubuti projected that the *Bulletin* would subsequently be sustained through subscribership. IPE leveraged space in the *Bulletin* to insert IPE perspectives into the tensions between Chicago's public schools and the

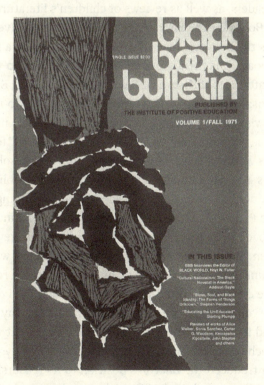

FIGURE 3.2. *Black Books Bulletin*'s inaugural issue, Fall 1971. Reprinted with permission from Third World Press Foundation.

Black community, calling out "abysmally low literacy rates" for Black children in Chicago Public Schools and asserting that these institutions cultivated a culture where "simple math is feared with a passion."[14] In the *Bulletin*'s special double issue on children and education, IPE argued that its existence was to "provide rays of hope and . . . be of positive service to our community . . . a resource-research community center, concentrating its efforts in the development of community-based programs that provide identity, purpose, and direction."[15]

If the vision of the Black Arts Movement was to invite everyday people into literate and literary spaces by making art accessible and explicitly political, the *Bulletin* worked to make this vision a reality through its journalistic engagement with ideas. The BBB Interviews section captured conversations between the editorial team and Black thinkers, scholars, and practitioners who were *not* the usual suspects among movement builders. Every issue carried reviews of literature across genres for mature readers, as well as reviews of children's literature in a section entitled "Books for the Young," which I discuss extensively in Chapter 4. Perhaps the best evidence of the journal serving as a metaphorical bulletin board was the annotated bibliography, "Biblio 1." Organized into the categories of Historical/Political/Social Studies; Biography; and Collections: Drama, Essays, Fiction and Poetry, "Biblio 1" highlighted what IPE visionaries were reading and perceived to be must-reads for the process of nation building. "News from Publishers" featured Black publishers worldwide; one issue dedicated this section solely to African publishers, bolstered by advertisements from Black publishers such as Jihad Productions in Newark, Drum and Spear in Washington, DC, and Broadside Press in Detroit. Later issues of the *Bulletin* included letters and feedback from readers and children's literature reviews written by children. The *Bulletin* refrained from telling readers what to do and how to think, but always offered many destination and route options.

Despite creating and editing the *Bulletin*, Madhubuti did not center his own work or ideas, often placing his editorial essay after leading essays and features. Using a straightforward voice that would characterize much of the journal's writing, Madhubuti's essay, "What We're About," introduced the *Bulletin*'s position to its readership.[16] Appearing twenty-five pages into the fifty-eight-page inaugural issue, this essay signaled the *Bulletin*'s desire to show readers—rather than tell them—IPE's worldviews and commitments. According to Madhubuti, the *Bulletin* was primarily focused on influencing Black community influencers across several domains:

> In our small way, THE BLACK BOOKS BULLETIN will try to supply positive information and images to black people who influence other black people, such as teachers (elementary, high school, college, etc.), postal workers, policemen, librarians, students, doctors, lawyers, dentists, nurses, writers, artists and others. It is premature to think that we can reach the masses of black people. We don't have the people, money, resources or time to do that, but we do feel that we can reach some of the people who influence and direct the lives of others.[17]

Madhubuti stressed the importance of positive information and images in the lives of Black people, whomever they were, wherever they may have been. He and other IPE visionaries understood that those who control the media and other institutions often wielded extreme power, and they were adamant that negative images and anti-Black messaging could be detrimental to Black children's identity development. It was in this vein that IPE often situated Black parents as ultimately responsible for their children's sense of self:

> We understand the positive and negative effects parents have on children (we're working on this), but we also understand the positive, but mainly negative effect teachers have on our children. Certain segments of the black community are now seeking community control of schools—that's fine, but it seems to us that if you have six thousand black teachers in a public school system (as in Chicago for example), you automatically have community control in many ways. The problem is, however, we don't have control over or influence over the minds of six thousand teachers now serving the system. Multiply this by fifty states and countless cities and at first the task seems insurmountable.[18]

Through the *Bulletin*, IPE redefined the concept of educator, expanding the network of stakeholders in children's lives. Their emphasis on influencers, as opposed to formal teachers in school settings, reframed the education of Black children as a collective movement. Schools in Chicago could not be expected to educate Black youth without the input of Black parents, educators, and community members. The seemingly "insurmountable" task of reaching thousands of teachers across Chicago alone sparked IPE and the *Bulletin* to do *their* part as influencers.

In his editorial, Madhubuti was careful not to romanticize the reach of IPE, the *Bulletin*, or any other IBI publication. IPE was always realistic about scale, seeking to have as much influence as they could muster in their part of the IBI constellation as possible. He maintained that a collective could, however, have some impact and influence over the spheres they were part of. Humility was at the heart of this introductory editorial. Closing the essay, Madhubuti invited readers to share critiques blurring boundaries between the editorial team and readers: "We need to know what you think—you are why we exist. . . . This is not a game to make a few people secure and popular—we are not about ego-tripping, cliquism or putting people down for the sake of personal aggrandizement."[19] A clear paradigm shift away from a solitary charismatic leader model and in pursuit of a new Black world they sought to realize, the *Bulletin*'s leadership mirrored IPE by nurturing a "collective orientation to leadership."[20] One way the IPE as an organization actively resisted elevating one voice and one idea over others was through their recurring section BBB Interviews, in which the editorial team engaged with Black thinkers from a range of backgrounds.

"Being Black Is Not Knowing Black": Conversations with the *Bulletin*

BBB Interviews was the *Bulletin*'s North Star. When the *Bulletin* was organized around a particular theme, BBB Interviews sometimes coincided with that theme. For example, comedian and activist Dick Gregory, who was also recognized as a health advocate for Black people, was interviewed for the "Heath and Black Survival" issue. Barbara Sizemore, the first Black woman to serve as superintendent of a major school system, was featured in the special issue "Children/Education." And, for a

FIGURE 3.3. Barbara Sizemore's interview appeared in *Black Books Bulletin*'s special double issue on children and education, Winter 1974. Reprinted with permission from Third World Press Foundation.

creative twist, the *Bulletin*'s special issue focused on history included a "created conversation" between W. E. B. Du Bois, Marcus Garvey, and Booker T. Washington.

Featured interviewees shared the common goal of equipping Black people with information, tools, and vision for robust and thriving futures. This required the examination of every aspect of Black life. As managing editor, Jabari Mahiri facilitated many of the interviews, and reading them feels like witnessing a conversation unfolding. He asserted that, through the journal, IPE visionaries "saw ourselves as documenting the best thinking of the most prominent cultural nationalists that were in the country at that time." Notably, the *Bulletin* did not fear tension or romanticize the Black experience or perspective as one unified idea. According to Mahiri, the *Bulletin* was a place to "harness" and "document ideas" and then "reflect those ideas back to the larger Black community."[21]

> We interviewed [Na'im Akbar]—major psychologist—at *Black Books Bulletin*. And we interviewed [Amiri] Baraka. So we were looking at all these people who were pushing on the cultural nationalist front. And, of course, if we go further back in time, the way that the Garvey Movement influenced the contemporary cultural nationalists of the seventies and eighties . . . the conflicts that Garvey and DuBois had with each other were also being manifested three decades later.[22]

The *Bulletin*'s editorial team did their best to ask interviewees challenging questions and prepared themselves for challenging responses. Their interview with Barbara Sizemore, Washington, DC, Superintendent of Public Schools, took place as she was navigating tensions in her leadership role. A native Chicagoan, Sizemore was raised in Terre Haute, Indiana, and completed her undergraduate studies at Northwestern and her PhD at the University of Chicago.[23] When asked her thoughts about the Black independent school movement, Sizemore had a frank response: "I just think it is a hopeless effort if it is not attached to the church . . . when you are trying to build a school you have to organize people for something. The strongest dynamic that [people] can organize [around] is religion and nationalism."[24] Sizemore discussed how both the Catholic church and the Nation of Islam synthesized beliefs, values, and education in their schools. Like most IBIs, IPE was decidedly not a religious institution, but the founders well understood the strong ties between Black communities and Black churches. The *Bulletin*'s team agreed that Sizemore had a point, and the interviewer responded, "but you know what the problem is . . ." without completing the thought, which seemed to prompt Sizemore to be even more straightforward:

> We have to get back in that church and do something about church response to the educational priorities of our people . . . I really think they are losing a golden opportunity. . . . It's hard but it would be a good idea in the long run. . . . I don't think we are going to get all our people together through

nationalism because I think that is harder. . . .You have so many people running around saying "I ain't no Afrikan" but you don't have too many people running around saying "I don't believe in Jesus." If they don't, they won't say it.[25]

Barbara Sizemore's interview illuminated some of the critiques of independent Black educational institutions. These schools would never be able to educate the number of Black children who were attending—and often being mis-educated—in US public schools. Therefore, IBI schools were sometimes viewed as operating in a bubble or occupying a niche market. Sizemore's interview also demonstrated IPE's willingness to use the pages of the *Bulletin* to process some of these tensions in a public forum and create space for ideas that both reflected and challenged their own views. Also, many African Americans did not refer to themselves as "Afric/kan" or align themselves with the Civil Rights struggle, at a time when Civil Rights and Black Power were presented as binaries.[26] In a influential study of independent black educational institutions, Russell Rickford asserted that "recognition of the limitations of culturalism led to the discrediting of cultural nationalism in the eyes of the Black radical intelligentsia" and that some characterized cultural nationalism as an "escapist ideology."[27] Yet, through the BBB Interviews section, IPE had a way to provide readers with concrete understandings of Black Cultural Nationalism: conversations with of the two of the movement's architects, Malauna Karenga and Amiri Baraka.

After Karenga conceptualized the Nguzo Saba, Baraka operationalized them in *Kawaida Studies: The New Nationalism*, published by Third World Press, making the concepts more accessible.[28] When the *Bulletin* featured Baraka in BBB Interviews, the team asked him about "ideological correctness." Referencing a recent confrontation between Karenga's US organization and the Black Panther Party, which had Marxist leanings, the team asked if Baraka was concerned that the Black Nationalist organization he had founded, the Congress of African People, could eventually fall prey to such conflict. Steadfast in his commitment to "struggle" with anyone committed to Black liberation, despite how they self-defined, Baraka responded: "That's why we specifically try to work with Black united fronts. . . . We are nationalists—revolutionary nationalists. We think the key to socialism is national liberation. But still we work with some people who think that the principle contradiction in America is imperialism and racism. We're still gonna struggle and work with them."[29]

Karenga, who was working on his doctorate at the time of the interview with the *Bulletin*, argued that Black people's liberation was contingent on liberating themselves from the "twin rule of racism and capitalism," offering a contrast to Baraka's interview. Karenga's approach to Black liberation focused on internal struggles. While economic and political struggles were certainly important, in Karenga's assessment of Black people's futures, he believed culture was the starting point for Black freedom and futures:

> The battle begins on the cultural level, regardless of wherever else it leads us. Culturally, we must, as we've always argued, begin the battle for the minds and hearts of our people, for if we lose this battle we can't hope to win any other one. The oppressor is inside us as well as outside us . . . commitment to bring into being a new world, woman, man, and child must come into being before they do. All real revolutions recognize this fundamental fact.[30]

Karenga's perspective of culture as the key battle ground to achieve Black freedom and autonomy may have been part of Sizemore's critique if IBIs. Sizemore found it farfetched, if not utterly impossible, that IBIs could organize masses of Black people in America around identifying as "Afrikan." Karenga, on the other hand, asserted, "We must stop confusing being and knowing; being Black is not knowing Black the way it needs to be known."[31] The *Bulletin*'s objective, to cultivate Black ideas and provide affirming images of Black people and Black life to Black families, not only aligned with Karenga's assertions of Blackness as a balance of color, culture, and consciousness, but signaled that futuring for Black lives had to be an intentional act in and by the Black community. Using the discourse of foresight, Karenga's vision for Black futures was obtainable if Black people chose to create it. In fact, Karenga suggested that the future would only be "unique" once Black people acquired "power and values to shape" their own image. Agency in the future would allow

Black people to "[enjoy] a free, fuller and higher level of human life."[32]

To be clear, though, interviews examining Black Cultural Nationalism did not overshadow the *Bulletin*'s foundation as a literary journal. BBB Interviews moved between writers, scholars, and practitioners throughout its tenure, and interviews with writers, publishers, musicians, and artists captured the intersectionalities of arts and politics, a defining value of the Black Arts Movement. Under the leadership of Hoyt Fuller, *Negro Digest / Black World* built an intellectual home for artists, writers, and thinkers, and a global stage for Black freedom struggles, for example. By his own admission, Madhubuti was among the Black leaders for whom Fuller clarified the potential of publications within the goals and processes of Black institution building. Central to winning the cultural movement, certainly, were Black poets, writers, thinkers, and publishers—because they could and did supply much-needed positive messaging. Publishing houses, performance spaces, studios, and other institutions were needed to keep Black ideas intact. In his *Bulletin* interview, Fuller was candid about his (first) departure, in 1957, from Johnson publications and "frustration" with *Ebony* magazine, which he deemed "irrelevant" to Black realities:

> It was the time of forced school "integration" and you'd pick up the paper every day and you'd listen to the news every day and white people were abusing black people all over this country pretty much the way they had been doing way back in 1919, just after World War I. . . . I couldn't stand working for this magazine which to me had great potential for making black people understand not only what was happening to them, but what was possible for them to do about it, and the magazine was not interested.[33]

Fuller's role in the Black Arts Movement has been largely understudied, according to scholar Jonathan Fenderson, who notes that "rarely out front or on stage in the limelight, Fuller occupied the background—a position that afforded him tremendous power and influence."[34] Upon return to Johnson Publications in 1969, again as editor of *Negro Digest*, Fuller orchestrated an activist movement to change that journal's title to *Black World*. Fenderson recounted Fuller's strategy to remain conspicuously at his desk throughout a protest he had organized outside in

December 1969—knowing the protesters would have more impact if he did not appear to be at the helm of the movement. Outside, the protesters demanded that Johnson Publications (1) stop using the term *Negro*, (2) promote (a renamed) *Negro Digest* to the same extent as Johnson's widely distributed *Ebony* and *Jet* magazines, and (3) engage Black people as models, authors, and advertisers across all Johnson publications. *Negro Digest* was renamed *Black World* in 1970, in response to the protest, and Fenderson points to the unique contributions of this journal under Fuller's leadership: "If the coupling of Black nationalism and art served as the ideological design for the Black Arts movement, *Negro Digest* provided the material evidence of an existing national network of individual artist, activists, and organizations . . . granting life to a collective sensibility."[35] When *Black World* was cancelled, echoes of Fuller's past critiques of Johnson Publications reverberated throughout Madhubuti's editorial "*Black World*: The Silencing of a Giant." Lamenting "the demise" of *Black World*, Madhubuti noted that the public announcement was hidden behind an announcement of Johnson Publications' "newest addition to white world fantasy—Fashion Fair," and that Fuller was subsequently fired "after seventeen years of service . . . without proper notice of due process."[36] *Black World*'s cancellation underscored the importance of shared values throughout an institution, which resonated strongly with IPE, where shared commitment to being positive influencers of Black people permeated all work.

Lastly, I note that BBB Interviews very intentionally revealed the books, journals, newspapers, and resources that interviewees were reading. In his interview with the *Bulletin*, Karenga talked about the "alternative thought" and "incisive brilliance" of *The Black Scholar* and *Review of Black Political Economy*, as well as publications coming from Institute of the Black World.[37] Pulitzer Prize–winning poet Gwendolyn Brooks discussed publications such as the *Liberator*, *Soulbook*, *Black World*, *Essence*, and *Ebony* when discussing the future of Black media. Brooks noted that "everybody buys or turns over the pages of *Essence* on the stand" but she read the *Journal of Black Poetry*, *The Black Scholar*, *Black World*, and *The Black Collegian*, which consistently inspired her to serve as editor for her own publication, *The Black Position* (1971–1974).[38] Reading was a necessary part of life and intertwined with a healthy lifestyle, according to IPE visionaries.

"If We Are to Be Free": Health and Wellness as a Destination

In fact, Black health and wellness had dedicated space throughout the *Bulletin*. Themed issues such as "Health and Black Survival," "The Black Family," "Meaningful Relationships," and two "Black Psychology" issues addressed health and wellness from the vantage point of what could be done to support thriving Black futures. Topics were often anchored by reviews of related books with contributors who ranged from emerging scholars and researchers across the country to practitioners in Chicago-based health and wellness centers. The *Bulletin*'s attention to wellness was an extension of IPE—where/whose educators and visionaries were immersed in many facets of operations and programming, and put in long days. Kimya Moyo talked extensively about raising her children at IPE and being able to stop and nurse them when needed. She even referenced a photo of her nursing one of her children that appeared within the *Bulletin* as part of an essay about the benefits of breastfeeding for mothers and babies. "Breastfeeding was kind of new," Moyo recalled, "it wasn't even as popular as it is today and that's not *that* popular . . . we were pushing breastfeeding." Moyo also explained that "food was important," and IPE thus had nutrition classes.[39] IPE co-founder and poet Johari Amini was viewed as a wise guide for healthy living by IPE visionaries. Amini introduced juicing and vegetarianism to the community: "You can't talk about building an institution if you're ill . . . if you're well you'll have the energy to withstand all that's needed. So, nutrition and health were an integral part of what we did."[40]

An emphasis on work, or "kazi," in Black institution building suggests that wellness was not necessarily a focus during the continued struggle for Black freedom. "Kazi (work) is the blackest of all" was a popular phrase repeated in songs and speeches. Even a letter in the Shule Juma-mose archives written to students by my mother ends with "Remember—Kazi is Blackest of all." This slogan, which was the 1972 Congress of African People conference theme, contributed to the "valorization of work."[41] IPE was not immune to the focus on work. Moyo and her husband were married in an IPE ceremony in a park down the street on a Sunday, and Moyo recalled returning to work at 7:00 a.m. on Monday, "It wasn't even about a honeymoon. I don't even know what that is. We

FIGURE 3.4. *Black Books Bulletin* dedicated the Summer 1975 issue, "Health and Black Survival," to issues of health in the Black community. Reprinted with permission from Third World Press Foundation.

rejected all of that. It was just about work.... Kazi is the [Blackest] of them all. Kazi means work." Moyo laughed, thinking about the songs that her fellow IPE visionary Soyini Walton created to make it easy to learn sayings and values. Kazi, through Moyo's lens, was an honor, and because IPE provided space for their workers to eat well, take a jog with colleagues during the day, breastfeed and take care of their own children while at IPE, her time at work and working felt fluid: "You have to recognize that institutions involve all parts of one's life. So when you go to work and you come home, that is not necessarily institution building because you are dividing yourself between wherever you are working. It is not providing everything for you. [When] you talk about institution building, then the institution must provide stuff for you."[42]

Health and wellness themes were approached in intersectional ways in the *Bulletin*. Coupling the notions of "health" and "Black survival," a 1975 special issue addressed a historical moment: the end of the Vietnam

War, US unemployment reaching 9.2 percent, and a recession. President Gerald Ford felt the need to admit, "I must say to you that the state of the union is not good."[43] This truth was no revelation for Black people, and the *Bulletin* suggested strategies for readers to care for themselves, under/despite this weight. BBB Interviews anchored this special issue, with comedian Dick Gregory leveraging the platform to spread and deepen awareness and activism. On July 4, 1974, Gregory started a run from Chicago to Washington, DC, designed to sharpen awareness regarding wasteful food and water practices that would negatively impact future generations. His starting point was the DuSable Museum, one of Chicago's most recognizable Black institutions, and the *Bulletin* featured a photo of Dr. Alvenia Fulton running alongside Gregory.[44] Dr. Fulton was a local leader whose South Side wellness center, Fultonia, was often advertised on the *Bulletin*'s back cover. A guide for those seeking improved health through fasting, Dr. Fulton advised many Black celebrities in the 1970s. Her book *Vegetarianism: Fact or Myth? Eating to Live*, was highly regarded by IPE and favorably reviewed in the *Bulletin*.

This was just one example of how the *Bulletin* introduced readers to non-mainstream, sometimes innovative, sometimes ancient, ways to care for themselves. An essay about spinal manipulation was leveraged as an indictment against the US healthcare system: "The healthcare system in the United States and other Western countries has developed in such a manner that the average person feels unable to successfully administer to the basic needs of his family—even minor aches and pains seem to require the use of drugs."[45]A photographic essay exploring t'ai chi ch'uan underscored "good health longevity, rejuvenation, and the curing of illness."[46] Black and white images of Black practitioners in various poses, and even a couple practicing together, stood out for Black readers who could potentially see themselves in these images. Other *Bulletin* contributors—doctors, nurses, community health workers, and advocates of alternative medicine products and pathways—had similar messages: Black people should align with, and see as integrated, Black values of nation building and mental and physical health. Community health advocate Dolores Robinson's essay about hypertension, a condition newly understood to be one of the deadliest conditions for people of African descent, was rounded out with personal observation: "I am convinced that the solution to the current health dilemma has to begin at home. Blacks, either individually or collectively, must become more health conscious." Robinson suggested abandoning "traditional" soul food, like chitterlings, and practices such as saving "bacon drippings." Ultimately, she attempted to appeal to readers with the question, "Why pass it on to your children who, in turn, will pass it on to theirs? At least give them a chance for a good healthy life."[47]

Wellness for the entire family was a theme throughout these special issues and the field of Black psychology was part of this conversation. Wade Nobles, an architect of Black psychology and professor emerita and director of the Africana Studies Department at San Francisco State, contributed an essay early in his career examining the role of Black psychology in the Black family. Nobles, already a research scientist at a community mental health center in California when this article was published, asserted that scholars examining Black families should actively resist using white families as "standard":

> We recognize that if we [Black people] are to be free [mentally], we must begin to conceive of ourselves in terms of our own integrity . . . that integrity or nature, we argue, is the sense of "Africanity." We contend, therefore, that the Black family can only be fully understood when it is conceived of as a unit or system deriving its primary characteristics, forms, and definition from its African nature.[48]

Black psychology was growing, as a field and worldview, and psychology scholars such as Na'im Akbar, Asa Hilliard, and Amos Wilson, as well as controversial psychiatrist Francis Cress Welsing, published in the *Bulletin*.[49] In one of two themed issues dedicated to Black psychology, Na'im Akbar was invited to define "Black psychology" and compare it to "White psychology." Akbar, who earned his PhD in clinical psychology from the University of Michigan and would go on to publish *Breaking the Chains of Psychological Slavery*, *The Community of Self*, and *Know Thy Self* with his own publishing company, acknowledged that "Black psychology" was initially a reaction to so-called "White" psychology, a "theoretical frame of reference which tends to view all people from the perspective of what is expected in middle class Caucasian people."[50]

Though still committed to countering structural racism and racist ideas, many Black psychologists later formed the Association of Black Psychologists and made an intentional shift away from (mid-1960s) notions of Black psychology as a "political answer to white psychology." Many IBI visionaries did continue to appreciate, however, Akbar and others' use of the term "Afrikan psychology" as "a positive statement ... the Afrikan perspective says that the foundation for Black behavior lies in its true and natural heritage in an Afrikan context," and Akbar was interviewed for the Bulletin.

Health and wellness included, for IPE visionaries, the education of Black children. The *Bulletin* leveraged one of its two themed issues on Black psychology to highlight tensions around IQ testing in education. Education researcher Asa Hilliard's provocative title "IQ Thinking as Catechism: Ethnic and Cultural Bias or Invalid Science?" set the tone. His essay then drew comparisons between believers in IQ testing and cults: "There is a cult in our schools. It is the cult of 'intelligence.' As with any cult, the followers take its 'truths' for granted. . . . It has a priesthood, who by the powers with which they have been anointed to perform, prophecy. They do not heal. They merely foretell the future. They read palms. They are fortune tellers. The true believers in education trust these prophets."[51]

Using catechism as a metaphor for education's fixation on children's IQ scores, Hilliard asserted that a "cult of intelligence" coveted too much power. IQ test results were being used to reify claims of Black inferiority and relegate Black children to the lowest rung on the academic ladder. Like other IBI schools, IPE's African-centered preschool, New Concept Development Center, took a decidedly different approach, positioning Black children, families, and communities as asset-based—with gifts that teachers and schools were responsible for unearthing.

Hilliard's framing of advocates of IQ testing as palm readers and fortune tellers conveyed the frustration Black parents and Black educators had with the norm of sorting and leveling students in ways that typically left Black children at the bottom. The essay offered historical context for the test, summarized what the test claimed to determine, and provided questions about the process as an entry point for a discussion. Ultimately, Hilliard called for empirical proof that the tests were "*useful* in education—useful in the sense that positive improvement can be linked to their use."[52] Other contributions about the psychological development of Black children and mental health in Black communities, written for educators and parents, bolstered Hilliard's arguments. Psychologist Amos Wilson, for example, whose work focused on the socialization of Black children, used the pages of the *Bulletin* to appeal to parents and teachers alike:

> We as a people must look at, study, and if necessary, rearrange our culture so that we can begin to get the maximum potential out of our children, and then we must begin to develop that potential. We as teachers have to change our curriculum approach and reorganize our school systems . . . if you can get the child motivated, get the child to maintain its curiosity, to a good extent the child will educate itself.[53]

Wilson focused primarily on what parents and teachers could do, rather than on critique of structures and systems that did or could negatively impact Black children; he was a featured contributor to the *Bulletin* and a guest in BBB Interviews who talked about intelligence as a "sociological definition" that Black people could control: "Intelligence has no meaning other than its relationship to a culture. We must define intelligence in terms of where we want to go as a people, and we must train our children in terms of exhibiting that intelligence."[54]

As these examples make clear, worldbuilding was not an abstract concept for IPE visionaries and staff, or to the constellation of thinkers who contributed to the *Bulletin*. Dedicated space to the ongoing review of children's literature, centered as a tool for nation building and worldbuilding, demonstrated the extent to which IPE visionaries believed that grappling with life's conundrums through literature with thoughtful, affirming, and creative images and messages would invite Black children to view themselves as contributors to their shared and future world. In the next chapter I examine Books for the Young, a recurring *Bulletin* section dedicated to the review of children's literature, and how the *Bulletin* positioned Black children as catalysts for the future.

CHAPTER 4

"There Is No Magic ... Except the Magic of Truth"

Nation Building with Books for the Young

A tale from the Bakongo tribe of the Congo River Basin, *The Magic Tree*, retold by Gerald McDermott in 1973, tells the story of Mavungu, a young man whose twin brother, Luemba, is favored by their mother.[1] When Mavungu can no longer withstand his secondary status, he leaves home, traveling by boat along the river until he reaches an impassable tree. Studying the tree's leaves, he hears "strange voices" speak to him and realizes each leaf is a person. One magical leaf person is a beautiful princess. She transforms Mavungu into a "joyful and strong" man fit to be her husband. In exchange for a better life, Mavungu takes a vow of silence such that "the source of his wealth and pleasure must always be hidden." Described as a tale of morality by its publisher, Henry Holt & Company, the children's literature version of *The Magic Tree* ends with Mavungu visiting his mother. There, he forgets "those who loved him," revealing his source of good fortune "to those who did not love him at all." The closing images make clear that Mavungu has lost everything; he stands isolated among a grove of trees.

The Magic Tree was just one of nearly 150 children's books reviewed on the pages of the *Bulletin*, over the course of a decade, in a recurring section called Books for the Young. In a perhaps unexpected departure

87

from the intellectual dialogue of the *Bulletin* overall—given that the journal was composed primarily of scholar and practitioner essays, theories, and critiques across disciplines, and interviews with prominent thinkers—IPE prioritized the formal, ongoing review of children's literature. Providing intergenerational continuity, both in the context of the *Bulletin*'s aims and for IPE entities overall, Books for the Young centered children's literature as a tangible nation-building tool that could be leveraged to shape young Black minds. A fascinating blueprint of and for futuring—the process of actively re-imagining, organizing, and planning for self-determined, proud, and healthy (current and future generation) life journeys—Books for the Young reviews centered Black children and engaged their adult caregivers as impactful builders of children's Identity, Purpose, and Direction. One way this was to be done, agreed IPE visionaries, was promotion of purposeful reading, as intergenerational practice and a crucial element of sustainable Black futures. According to Books for the Young reviewers, *The Magic Tree* fell short of such aims: "There must be something dynamic about *The Magic Tree*; my three-year-old son diligently asks to get involved with it every evening. But my enthusiasm about the book does not match his. I suspect, however, that the illustrations are largely responsible."[2]

Books for the Young consistently praised children's literature with art showcasing "vibrant colors" and "compelling design motifs" that encouraged a young reader to "linger and study the beauty of Afrikan expression." However, aesthetics and beauty, which *The Magic Tree* did have, were not sufficient for deepening the values, tools, and skills that IBIs and other Black Power and Black Arts movement visionaries considered indispensable to preparing the next generation: "But is beauty all we need in this time of struggle? No! Yet this book offers only that. This story, adapted by the artist from a traditional Congolese folktale, does not give us any positive direction giving ideas. In fact, it reinforces concepts that we must move away from."[3]

While other American families may have been reading stories to their children that were departures from on-the-ground realities, Books for the Young reviews suggested that Black children need literature with "positive direction giving ideas."[4] Not only did this retelling of a folktale fail to provide direction, according to the Books for the Young editorial team, but this retelling of a folktale potentially misguided young learners.

Several concerns were raised about how relationships were depicted in the story, including the twins' competition for their mother's affection, the mother favoring one child over another, and a child left to believe that magic was the only solution to their problems:

> Well—there is no such magic that will bring Afrikan people wealth and happiness overnight. Only long days and nights and many seasons of committed collective work will get us what we need. We must use stories to reinforce a work ethic. Furthermore, secrecy about something that is beneficial to all is unprogressive and should be discouraged. Knowledge has to be shared, as we wage our struggle *and* after we win. NO one person or small group could possibly have all the answers.[5]

In this chapter I discuss how children's literature, in the context of IBIs, and IPE in particular, was a pedagogic tool for nation building that affirmed, informed, and invited Black children to be/come active participants in a literate and literary community. The decision to include children's literature in the *Bulletin* embodied one of IPE's core values—children, like adults—must be critical, thoughtful, and curious readers. Books for the Young underscored the desirability and benefits of reading as a cultivated and carefully curated habit. Books for the Young reviews were a type of nation-building practice, a practice that parents, caregivers, and educators could implement immediately. First, I explore how Books for the Young positioned children's literature as a tangible tool and a liberatory apparatus serving to animate IPE's assertion that Black children needed affirming images and influences to support their positive identity development. Then I turn my attention to key themes reviewed favorably: nation building, aesthetics, accessibility, and disruption of any imaging or messaging or practice that reified Black stereotypes or rugged individualism (as opposed to collective work and responsibility, which *were* key themes).

"Who Controls Their Images?" The Need for Books for the Young

Many Black publications during the Black Power and Black Arts movements employed a "tell-it-like-it-is" tone, conveying a sense of urgency and fierce honesty that despite civil rights gains Black people continued to struggle in education, workforce, housing, healthcare, and other domains.[6] This straightforward tone could be found in the Books for the Young review section, as well as the *Bulletin* overall. Reviews were grounded in an unapologetic and unwavering commitment to protect Black children from stories, images, and tropes that undermined their humanity. Books for the Young focused primarily on books written by Black authors and for/about Black children, and on Black publishers like Third World Press. However, Books for the Young also reviewed books written by non-Black authors, including books published by more commercial publishing houses.

Books for the Young dedicated most of its space to books that affirmed Blackness, Black people, and Black wisdom and ways of being, but books with messages or images that could be problematic or even dangerous to young Black readers were also reviewed. Pedagogical critique of this kind provides parents, caregivers, and educators with resources for and practices of discernment, with respect to selecting literature for their children and students. In Chapter 3, IPE visionary Jabari Mahiri—managing editor for most of the *Bulletin*'s tenure—referred to the "brilliance" in Madhubuti's decision to include Books for the Young and to thus position Black children as exigent to the work of futuring for Black lives. Mahiri noted that the *Bulletin*'s treatment of children's literature distinguished the journal from other Black publications, and possibly inspired Chicago-based Johnson Publication Company to launch *Ebony Jr.* magazine, which had short stories and interactive activities for children.[7]

Throughout his writing and work, Madhubuti was consistent in his message that everything IPE did was about the children. Invoking the *Bulletin*'s aims to provide positive images to Black people and especially Black children, Madhubuti asserted "images shape and form our lives" and "you reflect that which influences you the most" in his inaugural editorial entitled "What We're About."[8] Madhubuti and the editorial team forecasted that images and imagery have the greatest impact—positive or negative—on the next generation and urged Black adults to take control of the images their children consumed, to cultivate self-love and pride.

Images shape and inform our lives. He who controls the images of the world generally controls the world. This is not fantasy, but fact. With the knowledge that a nine-year-old black girl seeks creation in trying to make her hair like the little white girls on the other side of the city tells us images work; or the young brother who insists he's a "negro now but he'll be white when he grows up" leaves us little room to feel comfortable in. The generation that we look toward to carry on the real task of building a nation are fast developing with few concrete or positive images of their own.[9]

Madhubuti's assertions preceded any discourse of "cultural relevance" and "cultural responsiveness" in education, reflecting IPE visionaries' ability to examine and respond to signals in post-Civil-Rights-Act 1970 that they saw pointing to only fragmented manifestations of equality. Indeed, despite narratives that Black people as a group were "moving on up," Black cultural nationalists and Black institution builders understood that affirming Black humanity, beauty, and culture is a worthwhile and very necessary long-term investment in/for Black children and the futures they imagine.[10] Technologies like the printing press and skills such as typesetting were futuring tools to position *Black Books Bulletin*, children's books, and other materials to serve IPE's larger mission of being a "resource-research community center."[11]

Blaxploitation films were gaining momentum in the 1970s, presenting over-the-top caricatures of hypersexualized and always confident Black men and women. Some Black people viewed these films as a sign of liberation, whereas others believed such a pattern "degraded its audiences who were subjected to the mockery of the aspirations of Black liberationists."[12] Artist Yaoundé Olu continued to illustrate IPE values and beliefs on the *Bulletin*'s pages. In one issue, one of Olu's editorial cartoons followed the Books for the Young review section. The cartoon depicts a small child, clad in an oversized fedora and the type of platform shoes often worn by Blaxploitation film characters. Walking confidently, with hands in bellbottom pants pockets, the child was dressed in a manner associated with pimps. Olu's editorial cartoon included a caption with the question "Who Controls *Their* Images?"[13] The strategic placement of this editorial cartoon following the Books for the Young review section reminded parents that they had the power to control the images their children encountered.

How might children respond to monolithic depictions of Black masculinity as cool, often violent, and focused on material things, and/or Black women presented as hypersexual, dependent, and submissive? This was the trope of Blaxploitation films. IPE offered clear countermessaging, consistent across all its publications. In the Black Pages pamphlet series, which often featured essays that had been published in the *Bulletin*, Kuumba Theatre Workshop's critique of the Blaxploitation genre was presented.[14] Kuumba Workshop was a local live theater organization that produced staged adaptations of Haki Madhubuti's poetry and prose. In their "political and cultural condemnation" of *Super Fly*—the film, the culture, and the lifestyle—Kuumba Workshop expressed concern for the valorization of drug culture in such films, asserting "there is nothing more cruel than to bring a child into the world a confirmed junkie the minute it emerges from its mother's womb" and lamenting the rising number of "baby addicts" in and beyond Chicago. Such films, according to Kuumba Workshop, are "destructive" because of potent "images" and/with a "lack of positive portrayal":

> This is the latest, but by no means only, bloodcurdling proof that dope is systematically destroying an entire generation of Black people. No single factor threatens (and can ensure) the enslavement of future generations of Blacks more so than dope. . . . Yet, despite the overwhelming devastation of this mass killer, the latest in a long succession of ripoff films (all of which take deadly aim at the minds of Black people) actually glorifies a dealer and advocates the use of dope.[15]

Kuumba Workshop's "condemnation" was not solely directed at one film, but expressed collective concern regarding the power of images and representations to shape and potentially disrupt the lives and well-being of generations of Black children. Olu's editorial cartoon was a not-so-subtle illustration of IPE's shared mission with other Black institution builders in Chicago, including Kuumba Workshop. IPE's values shaped the *Bulletin*'s mission of influencing the influencers of

Black people. Madhubuti's assertion in the *Bulletin*'s inaugural issue, "You are that which influences you the most, i.e., your parents, teachers, peer groups, gangs, social clubs, university of America, ABC, CBS, NBC, comic books, Shakespeare, or whatever."[16] Suggesting that imagining and planning for futures requires affirming images, Third World Press advertisements on the back of the *Bulletin* declared, "We also see the need to provide our children positive reflections of self so that the minds of our future can flower."

Into this opportunity, Books for the Young amplified the scholarly discussions and debates presented throughout the *Bulletin*, modeling how caregivers can find and use a wide array of on-ramps to theories and ideas worth exploring and/or pursuing. The path of its children ultimately determines or undermines the norms of a community, over time. Madhubuti thus argued "the need for an Afrikan education" to prepare young people for "future membership" in society: "The most important asset a people has is its young. Without children there is no continuation, there is no future. You cannot build a black nation or a world with just one generation: we need generations. We need a youth that can complete that which we start, a youth that can challenge the future we're bound for."[17] This quote was repurposed in IPE materials and featured on the cover of the *Bulletin*'s special issue on children and education. Reading, and being well-read, paid homage to one's ancestors—connecting with past worlds—and laid groundwork for more nuanced meaning making in fluid and complex sociopolitical moments, as well as one's ability to articulate and unpack coherent arguments and evidence.

Reading was also a portal to the future, preparing readers to plan for and execute preferred futures. The Black Power and Black Arts movements challenged and invited everyday people to read widely and deeply, to cultivate skills and critical thinking to "challenge the future we're bound for."[18] What better way to ensure a preferred future for Black people then investing in children's literate and literary trajectories? As seasoned futurists, IPE visionaries believed the future was tangible and something Black people could plan for and control through principled work. Doubling down regarding the need/call for parents and caregivers of all kinds to engage seriously with children's literature, IPE leveraged advertisements in the *Bulletin* to further its mission to cultivate readers with the statement: "What they read tells a lot about you."[19] Books for the Young's critique that *The Magic Tree* centers one person's good fortune, rather than family and community, and validates reliance on magic or luck from external sources, rather than intentional hard work and internal focus, reinforced IPE's aims to advance the struggle for Black freedom and futures "beyond the personal needs of one or two individuals to the needs and aspirations of the entire community."[20]

"We Are a Nation Becoming": Nation Building for the Young

At the other end of the spectrum from *The Magic Tree*, a coloring book titled *Children of Africa* was suggested as being aligned with self-determined, self-reliant futures. Excitement about *Children of Africa* was palpable in the opening line in the Books for the Young review: "Have your children take out their crayons, especially the deep colors like red, green, and black, and get ready to work in the most intense coloring book ever published. . . . I have nothing but praises for this book whose theme is Pan-Africanism and black unity."[21] The red, black, and green colors were a nod to the Pan-African flag adopted by Marcus Garvey's United Negro Improvement Association in 1920. The Books for the Young editorial team's assertion that this (or any) coloring book for children could be "intense" was just one example of review messaging in praise of literature and literary materials that integrated social and political context.

Children of Africa was far more ambitious than a traditional coloring book, presenting opportunities for Black children and those caring for them to engage—together—the values of self-determination, collective work, and responsibility. Books for the Young positioned *Children of Africa* as an expansive coloring book that "seeks to bring parent and child closer together."[22] The review endorsed the *Children of Africa* creators, who asserted that parents and guardians should be their children's first teachers and should actively resist outsourcing their children's education to so-called professionals.[23] Coloring pages on the right were accompanied with script for readers on the left, which contextualized each image. The readers' text is presented as neat, handwritten

FIGURE 4.1. "Books are fruit." Children at a Third World Press event. The bulletin board in the background has a tree with covers of books published by the Third World Press, while the table, surrounded by young readers, displays copies of Gwendolyn Brooks's *Report from Part One*. Reprinted with permission from K. Kofi Moyo.

script, in all caps, while lettering on the children's portions uses an artful block style, inviting children to spend as much time coloring the words as the pictures. Early images and passages mostly offered a picture of African socialism—community members working and creating together, children learning from elders—and moving into more subtle concepts such as the African diaspora, colonialism, and independence.[24]

Children of Africa reads like a journey and invites children and those with them to interface with moments of joy and simplicity ("They danced and sang. . . . They listened to stories"). Book users/audiences also experience disruption to this freedom and joy, about midway through the book. Opposite the outlines of North America, South America, and Africa, with smaller pieces of land and figures spaced apart from each other, is text for readers: "There came a time when Black people were scattered all over the world." This is the first time people in the book are situated as alone and disconnected from others. Figures on the coloring pages no longer have faces, and the sense of intimacy that was heretofore part of this coloring journey is no longer present. The script opposite this coloring page is noticeably longer, with the goal of supporting young learners to grow in their understandings of the notion of "diaspora," the "scattered" people of African descent:

> The independence of Africa and her people ended in the 15th century. Africa's people were kidnapped and forcibly scattered throughout the world. We were taken to Martinique, Dominica, Guadeloupe and Haiti by the French. To Cuba, Puerto Rico, Colombia, Venezuela, and Mexico by the Spanish. To Curaçao, Aruba and Surinam by the Dutch. To the United States, Guyana, Trinidad, and Barbados by the British. To Brazil and Portugal by the Portuguese.

Revelations of interconnectedness across time and space are punctuated by coloring pages with individual children in their new spaces—"Now in the West Indies there is Clara. . . . In West Africa there is Kofi. . . . In East Africa there is Opiyo. . . . In Chicago, there is Willie. . . . In Mississippi there is Mae"—to illustrate the scattering of African people that resulted in Black children existing in every part of the world. This section then does something more. Clara, Kofi, Opiyo, and Willie not only exist throughout the world but are inextricably linked in their struggles for self-determination and freedom. Now the world has Black children "like you," one of the final scripts for readers states, setting a rationale and tone for nation building at home and abroad, while offering a lesson on Pan-Africanism: "We often think that our interests and problems as a people are unique to the places in which we now live. So we view our interests as unique to the United States, or South Africa, or England. All over the world the interests and the problems of Black people are the same."[25]

This lesson, perhaps one for the adult reader as much as the novice, bridges IPE's work across all their entities, animating the *Bulletin*'s mission to include subjects "that affect Black people wherever they may be."[26] The favorable review of *Children of Africa* even included a flare of drama, "Get lots and lots of copies. . . . Buy out Drum and Spear so they'll have to reprint this many times," signaling that supporting Black publishing houses was consistent with, and even key to, nurturing young Black readers.[27] In addition to introducing Pan-Africanism and urging

There Is No Magic... · 97

the support of Black publishers, Books for the Young offered a window through which to view the culture of nation building, which, according to both Drum and Spear Press, the coloring book's publishers, should not be confused with Black people's individual achievements. Drum and Spear did raise a critique of the roll call of "the Mary McCloud Bethunes" and "Benjamin Bannekers" in the introductory pages to *Children of Africa*. Bethune, an educator and presidential advisor, established the Bethune-Cookman College in 1904. Banneker's story and contributions were undeniably important, as well. Born free on his parents' tobacco farm in 1731, he became a writer, mathematician, and astronomer.

Educating black children about Black history understandably started with "firsts" as foundation for hope around celebrating (and people of all skin tones seeing) Black brilliance and humanity. All the same, Drum and Spear Press was concerned that focusing on individual achievements "[fail] in giving our children total view and understanding of our situation as Black people."[28] Books for the Young reviews were also critical of the so-called usual suspects in children's literature, and consistently emphasized collective work that individuals contributed to, rather than hailing singular heroes of the Civil Rights movement. A review of Eloise Greenfield's children's biography *Rosa Parks*, for example, named appreciation for the author's treatment of Parks, who was "sometimes obscured in the shadow of Dr. King" and illumination of Parks's "brave and steadfast" character, as important modeling for Black children:

> the book reminds us of what can be accomplished when a determined group of people come together, as the Afrikan people of Montgomery did, make careful plans and persevere until a victory is won. If we can win small battles with such actions, which are examples of Umoja—unity, Ujima—collective work and responsibility, Nia—purpose, and Imani—faith; then just think of how these principles would work on a grander race-wide scale to achieve the ultimate goal of self-determination. We want our children not only to think about these principles but to live them.[29]

In the same issue, Books for the Young reviewed a children's biography, *Ray Charles*, noting that Charles's story was certainly worthy of retelling because of the many obstacles he overcame in his life to be able to eventually share his musical talents with the world. Becoming famous and making a lot of money should never be the end of the story, and Books for the Young reviewers acknowledged Charles's "strength" and the limitations of presenting "material wealth on an individual basis is not what we are striving for."[30] Again, because many biographies lacked depth in demonstrating how people worked together, but did usefully portray Black strength and perseverance and brilliance, critiques of biography were instructive. Celebrating individuals and individual achievements provides few tools for children to use as they navigate their own lives, and the elevation of a lone figure can diminish the power of community.

It was not surprising that the publishers of *Children of Africa*, Drum and Spear, were in alignment with the vision of IPE and other IBIs. Drum and Spear co-founders, Charlie Cobb, a former Student Nonviolent Coordinating Committee field secretary, and Jennifer Lawson, who also served as arts director and illustrator, were Drum and Spear's representatives in Tanzania. They worked with Tanzania Publishing House to translate *Children of Africa* into Kiswahili and republish it as *Watoto wa Afrika* in 1972.[31] Cobb also published with IPE in their Black Pages pamphlet series, offering reflections on traveling throughout Africa and cautioning Black Americans to avoid romanticizing their relationship to the continent. Rather, he urged Black Americans to work and struggle in Africa as they would in the United States.[32] *Children of Africa* was published at a time of deepening interest in moving beyond superficial, stereotypical, and racist depictions of the African continent and its people. Books for the Young advocated shifting from children's literature focused only on African animals and landscapes to the diversity of Africa's people, making this coloring book both timely and welcome.

Nation building extended beyond relationships between Black Americans and first- and second-generation Africans in the United States, and Black Africans on the continent of Africa. Books for the Young wanted to highlight children's literature with tangible goals for Black children. Their review of one book in particular, *I Want To Be*, published by Third World Press, admired the authors' use of photographs of Black children engaging in a range of occupations both well known (librarian, farmer, teacher) and less familiar (architect, botanist, geologist, and hydrologist).

There Is No Magic . . . · 99

These *I Want To Be* professions correspond to letters of the alphabet, a formula familiar in children's literature. In this case, however, each page reads like a chant or affirmation, "I want to be an urban planner . . . So that I can help plan where our schools, homes, hospitals, and factories should be built." Every single letter that represents a profession includes multiple rationales for the desire to pursue the line of work and every entry ends with, "I want to be a good [insert profession] . . . So I must learn mathematics, science, and the history of African people." *I Want To Be* suggested that to be "good" at anything required knowledge of these specific subjects, which Books for the Young affirmed:

> This idea is extremely important because it implies that no matter what our children want to be, there are certain basic fundamental things that we all as Afrikan people must know. Of these I would say that the most important is an accurate knowledge of our history and culture because without these we have no guarantee that the professions and skills we aspire to will be used in the interest of Afrikan people.[33]

Some reviews included names of members of the editorial team; *I Want to Be* was reviewed by the *Bulletin*'s managing editor, Jabari Mahiri, who in addition to reviewing the book favorably, acknowledged its shortcomings: "One question that will occur to the reader is . . . where is this Afrikan nation which needs all these professions that are depicted?" This "unavoidable" question, according to Mahiri's review, implies this so-called ideal world is not yet in existence:

> But it does not exist as of yet for we understand we are a nation becoming. We don't control any means of production; we don't control many farms and cities; we don't control waterways to build bridges across. These are the realities of our dependent condition. Because of these realities, however, *I Want To Be* can really be appreciated. It is apparent that if we want to change our condition of dependency we will have to be all of these things and more. *I Want To Be* must ultimately evolve into what we have become.[34]

Leveraging and adapting a popular alphabet book template allowed the authors of *I Want To Be* to merge developmentally appropriate literacy learning with seemingly complex nation-building concepts by breaking them down into the work and complementary tasks of nation builders.

Whereas the *Bulletin* offered an enthusiastic review of *I Want To Be*, the review of *ABCs of African History* was lukewarm.[35] *ABCs of African History* featured biographies with the names of notable Black figures corresponding with letters in the alphabet, accompanied by a poem and a photograph. In some ways, both *ABCs of African History* and *I Want To Be* disrupted stereotypes by providing Black children with images of Black people engaged in positive activities. However, *ABCs of African History* made success less tangible by elevating historical figures as examples of excellence and fortitude, rather than positioning children as (the) changemakers. Books for the Young noted the potential disconnect between the book's aims and young readers: "These poems are excellent and are the best part of the book. Other good points are that quite a few of the biographies are of little known but important people. Some of our children must be awfully bored by now, having heard the virtues of Frederick Douglass, Sojourner Truth, and Phillis Wheatley over and over again."[36]

Infused with wry humor and honesty about the trappings of lone Black history figures, the Books for the Young editorial team even suggested that the "virtues" featured in the usual suspects' stories, while admirable, were potentially dated. These Black history heroes were (and still are) overwhelmingly aligned with both Horatio Alger's bootstrap analogy and the master narrative of the American Dream. Their success was often depicted as the result of persistence, individual-level hard work, and sometimes white support/saviors. Advocating for more appropriately exacting history sharing and storytelling, Books for the Young asserted that vigorous reexamination of the past was in order: "It is very important that we provide, for our children, books that tell the history of black people in simple language. And, when I say history, I mean the story of economic, political, cultural, scientific, social and religious movements that shaped the lives of our people. I do not mean a book of biographies."[37]

Children of Africa and *I Want To Be* were two different experiences of/for exploring the Seven Principles of Blackness and the overarching theme of nation building. Both books embodied the aims of IPE and other IBIs to leverage children's literature for Black growth and well-being, and both offered a sense of the greater landscape of Black people and Black experiences. While *Children of Africa* addressed the historical and cultural continuity from the continent of Africa to the Americas, *I Wanna Be* focused on the futures of the next generations as nation builders—architects, farmers, geologists—were all children. IBIs such as The East in Brooklyn and Ahidiana in New Orleans also had alphabet readers. Kasisi Yusef Iman, a teacher from The East's Uhuru Sasa Shule, wrote *The Weusi Alfabeti*, which featured images from "the many Black publications we read in our school" opposite the featured letter used in a sentence. Y was for "Youth," while Z continued to build on the need for youth: "Z—is for their Zeal. Bringing forth a Black nation, you've got to have some zeal."[38] Using pages that mirrored lined writing paper for young children, *The Weusi Alfabeti* left space for young readers to copy the sentences or perhaps write sentences of their own. Two of the co-founders of the Ahidiana / Work Study Center created and published *Herufi: An Alphabet Reader* in house. *Herufi* used letters to introduce action words: "B—Build," "C—Create," and so on. For "G—Growth," an illustration of people shopping for healthy food with the word "Good" underneath was opposite another illustration of someone growing their own food with the word "Best." Every letter and word was chosen with great intention: "We are not trying to raise 'cute' (simply black and beautiful) children or 'smart' (high IQs) children who will feed into and become a part of the American system. . . . Power to our people must start with positive education for our children."[39]

"To the Heights of Our Joy": Beyond Stereotypes for the Young

Books for the Young captured the children's literature landscape of the early 1970s in the *Bulletin*'s inaugural issue: "With the emergence of the era of Black pride and the call from educators for more relevant reading material for Black youth, there came a flood of books on the market directed to the black youth."[40] These early calls for diversity in children's literature focused on the inclusion of Black characters. However, as early as 1971, IPE used the pages of Books for the Young to challenge this narrow focus. Merely inserting Black characters into conventional templates would not suffice:

> Initially, it appeared as though the same old racist readers were called back only to have some characters painted a darker hue. The same stale "white-picket-fence-with-dad-in-a-suit" stories prevailed. Later came the books with stories supposedly set in the environment of the black child. Although the scene moved from the suburbs to the city, most of these books still have a fairy-tale quality about them. Because who are they written by? White authors, that's who.[41]

Books for the Young launched in the inaugural issue of the *Bulletin* with review of a book the editorial team deemed "artificial" and "perceived in the mind of a racist." The editorial team stressed the urgent need for more high-quality books for Black children, offering nuanced and expansive characterizations of Black life and possibilities, and bluntly described Mary W. Sullivan's *Jokers Wild* as one of too many "poor attempts by a white writer to portray the world of Black people." In the opening pages of *Jokers Wild*, the author prefaces a collection of photos: "Many young people in these pictures are black, proud, and happy. They love to make music, just as the ones you will read about in *Jokers Wild*. Have you ever played any of these musical instruments?"[42] Readers learn that Jokers Wild is the name of a teen band created by the protagonist, Randy, and his friends. A nameless Black mother, described as "large and angry," disrupts band practice and inquires if the boys can rehearse at Randy's home. Randy indicates that his own mother is entertaining, showing off a new television she was able to purchase thanks to "Smiling Sam, the Credit Man." And, indeed, when Randy returns home he finds people in every corner of his home, including on his sleepy baby brother's cot. Randy's mother is incredulous and seems more interested in entertaining her friends than making sure her children get a good night's rest. According to the Books for the Young editorial team:

> The books is really kind of insulting. Randy, a black teenager, lives in a not-so-poor white suburb. As a newsboy, he gets bitten by a wealthy white man's dog and is due for a settlement. We are told that he sometimes sleeps

in a toolshed in the park (?) because his mother gives too many parties (??). His mother is portrayed as a very simple-minded woman who always spends her money with friends—leaving Randy to buy food for the family. The simple-minded mother is the author's device for linking Randy to the hard times of a slum youth. This is an artificial story perceived in the mind of a racist.[43]

Question marks in parentheses indicated IPE visionaries' confusion and utter disbelief. Tropes such as "angry," "large" Black women making purchases on credit and prioritizing partying over children's well-being fueled IPE's desire to not only be in control of what images Black children consumed but to create alternatives to negative images through the *Bulletin* and Third World Press. Sullivan's story of Randy fed culture and class wars throughout the United States, and certainly in Chicago. The "welfare queen" trope, manufactured in Chicago, became a talking point for politicians and a ploy to capture the imaginations of working-class white people while/by constructing an image of a lazy Black mother and missing father.[44] The writing in Books for the Young employed humor and sarcasm, noting "Miss Sullivan surely was a social worker before she became an author. How else could she have picked up some tidbits of phenomena of the black lifestyle to distort into a story?" Reviewers also seemed to be weary of the publishing company's credibility with education materials noting, "And wouldn't you know it? The book is published by Field Educational Publications, a subsidiary of Field Enterprises."[45] Field Enterprises monopolized Chicago's media including the *Chicago Sun-Times*, *World Book Encyclopedia*, and the *Chicago Daily News*.

For Books for the Young, critique was a form of pedagogy, providing tools for parents and caregivers to analyze children's literature and be able to differentiate themes, images, and messages that could be beneficial to Black children—how to build and create the world one wanted with concrete and specific skills—from themes, images, and messages that were hurtful. Toward that end, Books for the Young offered critiques of any writer whose work they believed reified harmful stereotypes, even if the authors were Black. One young adult book, *Teacup Full of Roses*, by Sharon Bell Mathis, tells the story of a Black family through Joe, a middle child, whose older brother, Paul, is drug addicted and whose younger brother, Davey, is talented and often ignored by their mother. Books for the Young reviewers describe Joe's character as "gentle, compassionate, and philosophical," with beauty in his "altruism," yet also notes: "The mother is a wild fabrication of the author; or, if you will, the character has not been fabricated well enough. Her neurotic adoration of her one son, and her unrealistic indifference to her other sons, is reminiscent of the tale Cinderella. Perhaps it is my naivete that prevents me from really believing that a black mother would be this cold towards two very good sons."[46]

This review was in stark contrast to a review in *The New York Times*, which asserted that Mathis "weaves her plots with sure authority and creates her characters with economy and veracity," and comparing her to Lorraine Hansberry.[47] These distinct reviews demonstrate the divergent lenses many IBIs had from mainstream institutions. In a different issue of the *Bulletin*, Mathis herself contributed "True/False Messages for the Black Child," an essay examining children's books "designed to document that Black is not desirable but ignorant, clownish, and pathetic."[48] Employing an unapologetic tone similar to Books for the Young and that of the *Bulletin* overall, Mathis critiqued some children's literature of the day, asserting that "Black characters seem to exist only to explain the goodness of white people."[49] The pedagogical critique, then, of Mathis's *Teacup Full of Roses* exemplified the extent to which the *Bulletin* and IPE remained committed to being consistent and accountable.

When Books for the Young reviewed another book by Mathis, *Listen for the Fig Tree*, the work ethic of the protagonist, Muffin, was lauded, with respect to her representation as a "proud and strong girl" navigating her own blindness and attempting to rescue her mother from the "clutches of alcoholism."[50] On the surface, this storyline seemed rather similar to other books that received robust evaluations that were not positive. In the case of Muffin, though, the Books for the Young review stressed that this character did not attempt to solve her problems, or her mother's problems, on her own but sought out family friends, clergy, and business owners, which "illustrate[d] the importance of Ujima, collective work and responsibility, which means that our brothers and sisters' problems become our problems and we must solve them together."

Listen for the Fig Tree and *Teacup Full of Roses* were both stories of struggle, and Books for the Young highlighted Mathis's ability to connect characters in the former with the Black value system and quest for Identity, Purpose, and Direction:

> It is the duty of the Black writer to portray and reflect images of our lives as Afrikan people from the depths of our despair to the heights of our joy. At the same time [they] should lead us to see that which is positive and beautiful about the way we live while also pointing out that which should be changed. A responsible Black writer will not only seek to entertain, but teach and enlighten as well. Sharon Bell Mathis has done her job.[51]

Books for the Young reviews were as concerned with portrayals of Africa and Africans as with depictions of Black American life. Reviews expressed a yearning for authors to do more than focus on the landscape of African countries. One case in point was the review of a "classic," *The Child's Story of the Negro*, written by African American school teacher Jane Dabney Shackelford in 1938, and reprinted in 1962. Shackelford was ahead of her time in that she attempted to provide a children's version of the history of Black people starting from life on the continent of Africa to the peculiar institution of slavery in the United States. Perhaps not unsurprisingly, given the first edition publication date, narrative regarding the enslavement of Black people contained troubling "happy slave" tropes ("After supper [slaves] were free to enjoy themselves. What happy times they had! Sometimes they would gather in one cabin and have a party").[52] Like W. E. B. Du Bois, Augustus Granville Dill, and Jessie Redmon Fauset with *The Brownies' Book: A Monthly Magazine for Children of the Sun*, Shackelford was part of a movement of Black teachers creating curriculum that reflected the African American experience and sought to provide Black children with images that reflected Black beauty and pride.[53] Asserting that *The Child's Story of the Negro* was "a classic in the purest form of a racist interpretation of black history," Books for the Young posited how difficult it was to "escape the racist overtones."[54] Beginning with the book's structural framing—"The Climate of Africa," "Plants and Animals," "Insect Life," "A Queer African Fish," "A Tree That Is the Staff of Life," "The Lord of the Jungle," and "Jumbo"), Books for the Young reviewers noted that Shackelford's focus on "climate, flora and fauna" completely ignored and erased African people from the story of Africa and contained factual inaccuracies. Books for the Young closed its review of *The Child's Story of the Negro* with a member of the editorial team's experience trying to "convince both children and adults" that she had, in fact, been "uncomfortably cold" during the evenings while traveling in Kenya. Shackelford's treatment of the "go-tos" of Black history such as Phillis Wheatly, Benjamin Banneker, Frederick Douglass, and George Washington Carver reflected the early stages of building a Black History curriculum—and Books for the Young was unyielding in its final assessment, recommending against putting the book "in the hands of a child ... because it is a very dangerous book."[55]

"What You Are . . . You Are": Beauty and Purpose for the Young

Beauty and aesthetics often draw children to stories, and Books for the Young certainly appreciated aesthetics that were warm, inviting, and purposeful. Stories written and illustrated by artist John Steptoe were consistently praised for attention to beauty and nuanced portrayals of Black life and feelings. Steptoe's *Stevie* was the first of four of his books to be reviewed in Books for the Young. In the first review, the editorial team attended to Steptoe's art career by noting he had been compared to French expressionist Georges Rouault, by "the white press." Rejecting such a comparison and calling it "unnecessary," the review asked, "When will whites quit trying to validate black art by matching it to western standards?"[56] On the back flap of the first printing of *Stevie*, Steptoe describes himself as "a painter and not yet an artist" who doesn't "just happen to be black."[57] Born in Brooklyn in 1950, Steptoe attended the High School of Art and Design in Manhattan and studied with African American oil painter Norman Lewis. The Books for the Young team described *Stevie* as "warm" and states that "the physical appearance alone can lure anyone to steal away for a while and explore what's between its covers."[58] While the visuals were important, there was also admiration for development of the protagonist, Stevie, an only child who gets jealous about a new "little brother" family friend, suddenly in his home. Stevie does all he can to be mean to the boy, and when the boy leaves permanently Stevie feels surprise at his emotions of yearning and missing his "little brother."

Much like contributors to other parts of the *Bulletin*, including interviewees featured in BBB Interviews, the *Bulletin* supported talented Black writers, scholars, and practitioners, often before they were fully appreciated in other institutions. Steptoe's career as a children's book author and illustrator was just getting started at the time of this early review, and his legacy continues today through the John Steptoe New Talent Award, which seeks to "affirm new talent and to offer visibility to excellence in writing and/or illustration."[59]

Steptoe was not the only children's literature author and illustrator who would later go on to receive widespread recognition for their work. Books by Eloise Greenfield and Lucille Clifton were frequently reviewed in Books for the Young and would later be considered essential reading for children, standing the test of time. These stories included powerful illustrations and sometimes photographs. Greenfield's *Childtimes: A Three Generational Memoir*, for example, used photographs from her family archive alongside halftone drawings by the artist Jerry Pinkney, and Books for the Young celebrated Greenfield's ability to tell her family's story with a "positive-realistic analysis on Black life in America at different time periods but totally from a child's perspective."[60]

Purpose beyond beauty and aesthetics was not a focus unique to IPE or the *Bulletin*. The Black Arts Movement was grounded in the discourse that art had to speak to the people, to mobilize, galvanize, and incite action. Aesthetics were thus only as important as the values they illuminated in the lives of Black people. The so-called Black Aesthetic was an "ethical stance" with elements of race memory, middle passage/diaspora, transmutation and synthesis, Blues/tone as meaning and memory, and an overall feeling that was simultaneously "contemporary and historical."[61] Addison Gayle Jr.'s groundbreaking edited volume *The Black Aesthetic* was a foundational text of essays that examined theory, justice, poetry, drama, and fiction across genres. Gayle's premise was that the 1960s signaled a new day for Black art with a focus on artists being self-defining and self-determined: "Each has his own idea of the

108 · FUTURING BLACK LIVES

Black Aesthetic . . . few, I believe, would argue with my assertion that the black artist, due to his historical position in America at the present time, is engaged in a war with this nation that will determine the future of black art."[62] Gayle noted in his introduction that "less than a decade ago," white editors compiled the anthologies of Black writers, or invited a Black writer (typically male) to pen an introduction. *The Black Aesthetic* was the "first of its kind," and Gayle hoped it would serve as an "incentive to young black critics to scan the pages of *The Black World* (*Negro Digest*), *Liberator Magazine, Soulbook, Journal of Negro Poetry, Amistad, Umbra* . . ." and to "anthologize" the next generation of Black artists.[63]

In addition to opportunities to highlight artists and authors who collaborated with skilled illustrators seeking to wrap beauty around important messages and both demonstrate and elicit a range of human emotions, one of the many benefits of having an independent publishing house connected with an IBI was the opportunity to put into action the theories and ideologies that guided the work of collective movement building. Third World Press, under the leadership of Haki Madhubuti, recognized the scarcity of children's literature with positive images and messaging, and did its part to change that dynamic for families, libraries, and classrooms by including children's books in their offerings. *Jackie*, for example, was described as a book "for black children, written by black people and *published* by black people."[64] Emphasizing "published," Books for the Young revealed that *Jackie* was the first children's book published by Third World Press. Jackie, the protagonist, is new to the neighborhood and "plays hard" with a group of boys who are established friends. Ahead of its time, Jackie's gender identity is not revealed early in the story and the boys who Jackie befriends assume Jackie to be a boy because of how Jackie engaged in their antics. On the first day of school after summer play has officially ended, Jackie presents as a girl, much to the boys' surprise. Reviewers find value in the "nimble cartoonish illustrations" by the author, Cheryl Jolly, and "simple sentences in large print" that make the book "readable" for young children, in keeping with readability and aesthetics as highly valued foci in Books for the Young reviews.

In 1974, the first Black Pulitzer Prize–winning poet, Gwendolyn Brooks, published a children's book entitled *The Tiger Who Wore White Gloves* with Third World Press. Brooks made the decision to move her work to a Black publisher as part of a conscious transition from "Negro poet" to "Black poet."[65] In a Books for the Young review, the editor opened with "Is this our Sister Gwen? Indeed, it is. Acknowledging her Afrikaness and sending out powerful, positive messages to our children—our future?"[66] Tiger, who has "stripes of fierce black," feels as if these stripes are not stylish enough and decides to adorn himself in a top hat, cane, and white gloves. Amused by the sight of the tiger in these accessories, fellow animals ridicule Tiger, compelling him to rethink the decision to cover his black stripes. Books for the Young editors underscore this theme using rhetorical questions, "Can you imagine that? Remind you of us? Never satisfied with being ourselves!"[67] While acknowledging that Brooks was playing with the theme of identity, the editors posit that she is subtle and "the book may need some explanation." Though it is not entirely clear whether it is children or their adult readers who would need more clarification about the theme, the Books for the Young team offered their own analysis:

> In a time when we, as a people, are rediscovering and redefining ourselves, a strong reinforcement of our identity for our children is needed. Sister Brooks provides a portion of that reinforcement with this book. The Tiger found out how foolish he was to try to be something he was not by dawning white gloves. We, as Afrikan people, must make this foremost in our lives. We can't change ourselves by "acting" different or hiding what we are or by wearing "white gloves." This we must teach our children. In the words of the good sister, "What you are you are."[68]

Books for the Young created a bridge between IPE values and visions for Black children with tangible on-ramps to reinforcement of those values for Black children and their caregivers alike, using the medium of children's literature. Managing editor of the *Bulletin* and frequent contributor to Books for the Young Jabari Mahiri posited, "The basic [guiding question] under the umbrella of the Institute of Positive Education was what would be positive images, ideas, information, and representations for young children who are gaining their sense of identity themselves, their sense of themselves from the images that they're engaging through the children's literature?"[69] As one of the authors whose work was reviewed in Books for the Young, Mahiri asserted that while his book wasn't "ostensibly trying to be political," he was intentional about writing a story "reflecting cultural experiences." His book, *The Day They Stole Letter J*, weaves together Haitian culture, West African griot traditions, and African American traditions of community, with the neighborhood barber and elder serving as a storyteller: "It's about taking ownership for your actions . . . and the final line says, 'You don't have to fear power if you know how to use it.' The idea of young people seeing themselves coming into their own power but having a responsibility associated with their power are the residual implications of the book."[70]

Ultimately, Books for the Young signaled a "new day," to borrow from Sonia Sanchez's children's book published by Broadside Press in Detroit, and the pursuit of nation building in, through, and around children's literature often addressed parent/family/adult involvement in reading and values that should be present in choosing and discussing literature.[71] Children's literature that emerged from the Black Power and Black Arts movements provided some context for the "new Black"— that is, understandings of Blackness as more than color, and specifically as an opportunity to think and build collectively. Magic and fantasy may have been discouraged and some may wonder if the literature elevated by *Black Books Bulletin* placed too much burden on young readers, yet Books for the Young reviews suggested that the key to joy was positive reflections of Black lives and futures. That there was a joy to struggle— especially if the outcome was a better life for your family and community—and in responsibility and in defining oneself.

CHAPTER 5

"The Present Passes ... the Next Day—Mars"

Futuring for Black Lives

> And what was exciting was to know that we were building all of this at the same time something was being built in Sacramento ... at the same time something was being built in Detroit ... something was being built at The East in New York.
>
> **—KIMYA MOYO**

> The institution is not the building that the Third World Press exists in today. The institution is all the connections, because that brick, the bricks of those buildings, is each one of us, and the artists and the poets and the playwrights and the dramatists, all of that builds the institution.
>
> **—SOYINI WALTON**

Carol D. Lee was the first to arrive. I had reached out to IPE visionaries prior to the American Educational Researcher Association annual meeting in Chicago in 2022, and we had scheduled a late lunch between sessions. One of those sessions was a symposium examining independent Black education movements that I had organized, which featured Carol as a discussant. For the lunch, we were joined by Jabari Mahiri, one of his daughters, and his best friend from high school. It was a reunion of sorts, with Jabari's daughter meeting her father's comrades for the first time as a young adult. While Carol knew his sons well because

111

112 · FUTURING BLACK LIVES

they had attended IPE's preschool, she had not seen Jabari's daughter since she was a little girl. Carol peered over her glasses, checking her out from head to toe and giving that signature smile visible in the IPE Baraza ya Kazi image (fig. I.1), in which she is looking over her fellow builders and the babies on their laps. Carrissah, one of my graduate student researchers, arrived next, and excitedly introduced herself with gratitude to finally meet some of the visionaries whose interview transcripts and primary source materials she had helped me organize. Last, and certainly not least, Haki Madhubuti arrived, bearing newly printed copies of Jabari's children's book *The Day They Stole the Letter J*, which had been published by Third World Press in 1981 and reviewed in *Black Books Bulletin*'s Books for the Young in its final quarterly volume. When I interviewed Jabari the previous year, he noted that this book made him "feel more like an author" than all his academic works combined. "I have twenty-five copies for you here and seventy-five more at the Press. One hundred total," Haki said to Jabari, punctuated by a strong embrace. I imagined them—still Don L. Lee and Cleve Washington—finalizing paperwork to purchase a small farm in Michigan on behalf of IPE, when the banker had proclaimed, "Lee and Washington! Two of our famous generals!"[1]

Haki would later tell me that while Carol and Jabari crossed paths frequently in the education research world, he had not seen Jabari in more than twenty years. Smiles and laughter abounded as Carol began to share some IPE stories with Jabari's daughter, including the fun fact that her dad had officiated Haki and Carol's wedding. Haki joined Carol's chorus: "Your father was integral to Third World Press, *Black Books Bulletin*, and IPE." He and Jabari teased each other incessantly, like only dear friends can, with Jabari narrating the exchange, "And this is what we call 'signifying' in the Black community," inciting even more laughter.

It did not take long, though, for the table where we were gathered to become quite serious, with Jabari sharing, "You see, a bunch of us met Haki—he was Don L. Lee—at UIC. I was fresh out of the military, and he was introducing us to Black literature. He invited us to come the Institute [of Positive Education] and that's how I got involved." Jabari went on to say that Carol "ran the schools—that's why they were so successful." Everyone began to acknowledge Johari Amini, Soyini Walton, Kimya Moyo, and others unable to join us—raising up their crucial contributions to IPE efforts. Keeping with the tradition of shared leadership and Carol's notion of "commitment to the collective," Carol, Jabari, and Haki focused on the work of the group, rather than individual roles.

It was not long before everyone turned to me for a "synopsis" of my work and asked, "What are you learning?" I noted that the question posed was not "What did you learn?" We all acknowledged that learning from and with IPE visionaries and Black institution builders was and is unceasing. In this closing chapter, I aim to share what I'm learning from IPE visionaries and Black institution builders, with the understanding that there are many more stories to be recovered and opportunities in/with formally recognized and as-yet-undiscovered archives. My desire here is to generate some ideas about how IPE's futuring—largely created, disseminated, and sustained through print culture—left a record that continues to hold relevance and inspiration for those who seek to learn from, be informed by, and build on enduring legacies of "correct Black education." I also contemplate how IBIs that no longer exist as brick-and-mortar entities engaged in other acts of futuring that also contribute to these legacies. And, finally, I attempt to distill some of the salient characteristics of futuring that I have learned and am learning from IPE visionaries with relevance for cultivating mindsets and stances around and for designing participatory learning communities with equity in mind.

Toward this end, I consider how Historiography for the Future and my use of the Shule Jumamose Archive function as both method and methodology.[2] As method, Historiography for the Future uses historical case studies as a way to foreground contemporary conversations around equity work—and I am not the only scholar of African American education and African American studies to have considered the role of historiography in thinking about current tensions and possibilities in and for Black lives.[3] As methodology, Historiography for the Future entails collecting historical signals, rather than relying only on current innovations in futures and foresight work, and undertakes to reclaim archival work in/from formal institutions as well as sites yet to be discovered.

"We Worked Collectively": Legacies of Futuring

One of the topics IPE visionaries and I pondered during our late lunch in Chicago was the notion of sustainability and continuity. When IPE made the decision to pivot to a charter school model for their K through 8 program—and created Betty Shabazz International Charter Schools— the Council of Independent Black Institutions was critical of the move. Worth Kamili Hayes begins his examination of Chicago's "Golden Age" in education, when a wealth of private education options were available to Black families, with a story of mounting tensions around IPE's decision that the elementary program of their existing African-centered preschool and elementary school, New Concept Development Center, would shift to a charter model, noting that "several fellow Afrocentric educators responded with condemnation."[4]

Haki Madhubuti had a very clear stance, when we revisited this contentious moment between IPE and the Council of Independent Black Institutions. "That's our tax money!" he declared, noting that it was not "logical in terms of maintaining" for IPE not to make the pivot. A deeper dive into how IPE visionaries self-situated in a local and national constellation of Black institution builders shows that they always did things their way. "We need a historical record to talk about different ideologies," Carol D. Lee opined. For example, IPE did not align with the work of the Black Panthers locally, as they were "too involved with Marxism." IPE also broke with the Congress of African People in 1974, despite the truth that they "loved [Amiri] Baraka," yet they understood themselves to be "fundamentally different."[5] Jabari Mahiri gave a hypothetical example, "If we were at this table with Imamu [Baraka], his people would have to show deference while speaking." In stark contrast, Mahiri noted that when IPE had planning meetings for the *Bulletin*, the leadership rotated so each issue had a new direction. The *Bulletin* thus became a vehicle through which IPE leaders practiced the Seven Principles of Blackness with public accountability.

IPE's institutional commitment to use arts and literary arts as a prism through which to view the work of Black self-determination and self-reliance was largely due to Haki Madhubuti's own influence as a poet, writer, and publisher with visibility and reach in the Black Arts Movement—yet he did not position himself as the center. Carol D. Lee echoed this sentiment, asserting, "We worked collectively. . . . Haki never allowed us to develop a cult of personality around him. . . . [The Congress of African People was] top down and we weren't [saying] 'Haki [is] the great leader for us.' Haki was a member of the group we made." No one at IPE, including Haki, was above critiquing or questioning, though Lee noted that "part of his gift is his ability to get people to do the stuff he wants."[6]

I have no wish to paint a utopian picture of IPE, or IBIs in general, though note that whereas gendered labor critiques are widely documented, little attention has been given to how IBI stakeholders sought to redistribute workloads.[7] My archival and interview data show that tensions and challenges were often transformed into opportunities. By the time IPE chose to pivot to a charter school model and make other changes to their infrastructure, they were several steps ahead of other charter schools. IPE visionaries seemed willing to be unpopular when they believed their decisions would ultimately be in the interests of Black people. "Blackness is one angle," Haki asserted, "that's our angle. Our institutions will live beyond me and my wife. We dedicated our lives to Black people."[8]

Colleagues and comrades of IPE visionaries also dedicated their lives and life work to Black people. The East, for example, closed its doors in 1986, yet their presence continues to be felt. Brooklyn's International African Arts Festival—a festival started as the African Street Carnival, a block party organized by Uhuru Sasa Shule's parent council to celebrate the school's first graduating class in 1971—continues to be a site of Black culture of/for the past, present, and future.[9] In 2022, Tayo Giwa and Cynthia Gordy Giwa, Black business owners and curators of Black business history and information in Brooklyn, produced a documentary, "The Sun Rises in the East," telling the story of that IBI through its co-founders, former students, teachers, and parents, as well as footage of interviews with Jitu Weusi.[10] At one point in the film, a former Uhuru Sasa student declares, "We were the original Wakanda children," a nod to Ryan Coogler's cinematic reimagining of the Black Panther and futuristic vision of Black life on the continent of Africa and in the United States.[11] Giwa and Giwa are co-founders of Black-Owned Brooklyn, which includes a website and Instagram account "documenting Black life, past and present" in the borough, while seeking to cultivate "creativity, joy, and self-determination."[12] These leaders' acts of futuring are direct responses to gentrification in Brooklyn that they argue has "erased" stories and histories of Black ownership. Giwa and Giwa created a discussion guide that can be used by school and community groups to complement the documentary and facilitate its use

116 · FUTURING BLACK LIVES

as a starting point for dialogue. Organized in sections dedicated to each of the Seven Principles of Blackness, the activity for Ujamaa (Cooperative Economics) included analysis of The East's newspaper, *Black News*, along with other primary source materials.[13]

Like The East, New Orleans-based Ahidiana Work/Study Center continues to provide maps of the future, despite officially closing in 1988. Ahidiana's institutional commitments to Black futures remain intact and available to future generations in/via an online archive that includes PDFs of their *Operating Manual* (see Chapter 1), school brochures, pamphlets, and some of the books issued by their publishing company, including a children's alphabet reader (see Chapter 4). Co-founders and former teachers penned "Remembrances," offering the public some of their reflections on their work. "Memories of Ahidiana come floating back to me as I read these publications and essays," begins Tayari kwa Salaam's remembrance guiding sojourners through the IBI's publications and connecting the digital dots of the online archive. Kwa Salaam's final assertion—that the "successes" of their IBI are best seen in the "youth who grew up to be conscious, peace-loving world citizens"—contrasts with narratives that situate educational success as centered in grade point averages and test scores.[14]

When I asked Carol D. Lee about what she saw as the enduring contribution and legacy IPE offered through its publications, schools, and work in the community, she too, focused on children and their well-being and identity:[15]

> And [our students] have all turned out, without exception, to be good human beings, to love Black people, to see themselves as citizens of the world, for whom the idea of Black inferiority . . . is a silly, absurd idea that doesn't enter into how they see themselves in the world. And so the contribution, it seems to me, of their participation in these institutions—along with their parents, because we still have these long-term relationships with parents—was the development of whole human beings.[16]

Notably, both Tayari kwa Salaam and Carol D. Lee emphasized the importance of "world citizens" and "citizens of the world," affirming that their institution-building efforts, rooted in Pan-Africanism and global solidarity with marginalized and oppressed people throughout the world, are key measures and impacts of their work. I think of these continued manifestations of futuring as ways to "expand the lens"—to borrow from Kimya Moyo (see Chapter 1)—offering models for documentation and continued accountability in the work of futuring for Black lives and for equity and human thriving.

"We Functioned as a Village": Values of Futuring

One might (re)consider the notion of sustainability and the meaning of IBI innovations and pedagogical commitments as important to larger conversations about pursuits of equity and justice in contemporary education contexts. I have uncovered some core values of futuring for equity and for thriving Black lives that shaped Black institution-building efforts around education. Among these are being intentional, having willingness to struggle, valuing intergenerational and communal spaces, practicing shared leadership, being realistic about scale, and reimagining rather than reacting. Being "intentional" was a value named by IPE visionaries. For example, IPE math educator Kimya Moyo underscored that everything Black institution builders did, and how they did it, had to be intentional: "Given the crisis we are in as a people, it is a luxury to just flamboyantly do anything. . . . We have to be intentional about everything from what we put on to how silent it is you make a statement under your breath . . . everything we do has a repercussion."[17]

According to Haki Madhubuti, intentionality was/is a decision that should not be confused with the notion of "sacrifice." Being intentional, for IBI visionaries and builders, required constant thought and thoughtfulness, and in practice, often aligned with willingness to struggle. In the context of the Black Power and Black Arts movements, the ability to struggle was an honor, especially if the struggle related to educating the children and community. This message permeated the fabric of IBIs and their schools.

Black institution builders valued establishing and working in intergenerational and communal spaces. Elders, children, and everyone in between was invited to learn from and with each other. Pulitzer Prize-winning poet Gwendolyn Brooks was considered an IPE elder, and

Jabari Mahiri referred to her as a "patron saint" for IPE visionaries, who sought her wisdom around creating writing communities for young people. Figure I.1, of IPE's Baraza ya Kazi, captures the intergenerational and communal ethos of IPE's work, and what Soyini Walton refers to as the IPE "village": "We functioned as a village, per se, because you see all the babies in the laps. They are sitting on laps that weren't their [biological] parents but we all cared for the children and felt that they were our children. And it was just a warm time of building, a time of hope, a time of unlimited possibilities."[18]

An intergenerational "commitment to the collective" anchored IPE visionaries in their struggle to educate and socialize Black children for the future, and they enacted that struggle and their successes through foundational practices of shared leadership. IPE actively sought to include the work and voices of all stakeholders. Leadership in the planning and strategy meetings for IPE's schools and *Black Books Bulletin* journal publications rotated weekly. When parents expressed interest or curiosity in the Baraza ya Kazi, IPE co-founders and visionaries made sure they had a seat at the table. Men were expected to share in the work of educating young children and cultivate relationships with those children as much as women. IPE visionaries speculate that a key factor in their institution's longevity was the shared leadership model.

IPE visionaries talked often about being realistic about scale. Even the first issue of the *Bulletin* (see Chapter 3) asserted, "In our small way . . ." IPE hoped to influence influencers, especially those who interacted with Black children. Haki Madhubuti noted in that inaugural issue that while reaching the masses of educators and teachers, even in Chicago alone, was not attainable, the journal could move the needle by supplying "positive information and images to black people who influence other black people." Through the content and design and goals of the *Bulletin*, IPE visionaries communicated their desire to influence their part of the world and encouraged Black people "wherever they may be" to influence their own communities.

Lastly, IPE visionaries focused on reimagining—not reacting. There was no time to wait for the world to normalize conditions Black families needed or for local politicians to generate strategies that would strengthen Chicago's Black community. IPE and other Black institution builders created their own world. It is in the process of reimagining that futuring can thrive. How do IPE visionaries feel about futuring? "I don't see life in any other lens," Kimya Moyo exclaimed, when I shared my vision for Historiography for the Future and this work. In fact, IPE visionaries always dreamed about, planned for, and executed futures, as underscored by Haki Madhubuti, who told me: "Well, it's all about the future. The present passes, because the present is one day, boom. They next day, Mars, the future."[19]

EPILOGUE

"We Are Not Revolutionaries. We Are Farmers."

A Lyft dropped my family at Third World Press on a surprisingly sunny Friday morning on the South Side of Chicago, in front of a stoic building with Catholic church architecture. Bright blue awnings over every window assure visitors all is well in the building. Gold lettering across each awning honors the entities within: Third World Press, Third World Press Foundation, Institute of Positive Education, New Concept School, Betty Shabazz International Charter Schools, and Gwendolyn Brooks Writers House. Baba Shannon Sundiata Mason, the *mkuu* (principal, in Swahili) of Betty Shabazz academy, greeted us warmly, wearing a suit accented with Kente cloth. With tall stature, gentle voice, and deep eye contact, he intentionally leaned forward to lock eyes with both of my sons (then in grades 6 and 4) and shake their hands.

Baba Sundiata pointed out the area in front of Third World Press where, in December 2022, workers had to dig a large ditch to repair underground pipes that had burst and caused a devastating flood costing hundreds of thousands of dollars in damage. Ironically, that flood occurred just months after Third World Press celebrated a wonderful series of fifty-fifth anniversary events, and during one of its most important seasons, Kwanzaa. An outpouring of community support via GoFundMe exceeded the fundraising goal and included messages from fellow institution builders, scholars, and writers such as Malauna

Karenga ("Continue the struggle, keep the faith and hold the line"), Wade Nobles ("The liberation of the African mind is The Revolution we must win"), and Ishmael Reed ("Being a Black businessman in a country that's opposed to Blacks acquiring assets is a hardship. Especially if the product is thought").

As Shabazz students gave us a tour of their school, their pride and joy was palpable—though this task of hospitality and sharing was doubtless interfering with their official spring break. The sincerity was infectious. My sons were particularly wide-eyed when these children carried the Pan-African flag alongside the US flag, and made a powerful pledge:

> We are African People,
> Determined to achieve political and economic capacity.
> We are preparing leaders . . . and workers . . . to bring about
>   a positive change for ourselves . . . our families . . . and our
>   neighborhoods.
> We stress the development of our bodies . . . our minds . . . souls . . .
>   and consciousness.
> Our commitment is to sustainable living, self-determination . . .
>   and self-respect.
> Toward the building of a better community . . . a better nation . . .
>   and a better world.

We extended right fists, as instructed, before completing the pledge and moving into "Praise the Red, the Black, and the Green." My children's favorite part appeared to be "The Nguzo Saba Chant," as they were more than familiar with the Seven Principles. Later, they told me how "cool" it was that elements from "home" can be a part of a "school" routine.

The school staff made us feel like family instantly. There was a generosity of spirit that was infectious. One teacher made us smoothies as another discussed the freedom children experienced in the gymnastics and tumbling class. There was something to capture the imagination of every learner, with educators who were excited about preparing children to be confident not only in this world but beyond. This pattern was evidenced in Baba Sundiata's declaration: "We are not revolutionaries . . . We are farmers." As he pointed out that what we were seeing

Epilogue · 123

was part of daily practice and ritual, I could hear Madhubuti's assertion that the Institute of Positive Education was a "decision" to invest in the lives of Black children and their families. I also heard echoes of Kimya Moyo's insistence that everything a Black institution builder did was enactment of intention. Baba Sundiata continued, "We plant seeds." True, indeed—in the art on the walls, the messages, the symbols representing the "Virtues of Ma'at," and the Nguzo Saba throughout the school. Before we left the building, members of the Betty Shabazz International Charter School community gave me a copy of their handbook. The school's "Recommended Reading List" included titles mentioned during my interviews with Institute of Positive Education visionaries, published by Third World Press, reviewed by *Black Books Bulletin*, or authored by changemakers who were formally interviewed by, or otherwise contributed to, the journal. However, it was their pledge that remained with me.

> For the use of our power,
> For the triumph over our struggles,
> I pledge . . . my total devotion,
> To develop—fully our communities.
> I pledge . . . to study and do homework,
> I pledge . . . to lead a principled life,
> Exampled by the Virtues of Ma'at . . . and the Nguzo Saba.[1]

Acknowledgments

I knew I wanted to be a scholar when I had the opportunity to hear my father, James Fisher, give a talk entitled "Willie Brown as a Metaphor for the Black Route West." We were at the Black Route West Conference, hosted by the African American Studies Department at the University of California, Davis in 1995. Just one year prior, I had earned a BA in English from that school, with a minor in African American Studies. At the time of the conference, I was completing my teaching credential and planned to teach elementary school. There was one small problem with my desire to become a scholar, laughable now that I'm a professor. I was terrified of public speaking. And I was mesmerized by my dad's command of that space and his ability to speak with passion about his research and about his family's migration story. Recounting his mother's decision to leave Wharton, Texas, in the 1940s—where her children would have had to pick cotton during the school year, he remembered arriving in California and thinking, "We are as far West as we can go . . . our backs are against the Pacific Ocean." My grandmother Hallie had a similar migration story; it remains part of our family history and our shared future.

I want, first thing, to convey profound reverence to my parents. The late Cheryl A. Fisher was an institution builder and tireless lover of Black people. My father, the late Dr. James Fisher, is the constant gardener in my life and the lives of my children, reminding us to remain rooted in identity, purpose, and direction. My brother, Damany, and I count ourselves among the truly fortunate—raised in a home that affirmed our Blackness in ways that held us accountable to our community and allowed us to be citizens of the world. Prior to his passing, my dad read through this manuscript and offered invaluable feedback that not only strengthened it but planted seeds for future work.

From my first meeting with my editor, Gianna Mosser, Vanderbilt University Press was the right home for this book, and Gianna one of the best intellectual sparring and thought partners. Her patience and unwavering commitment to the work got me across the finish line.

Futuring Black Lives would not be possible without the generosity of Black institution builders throughout the United Sates, especially in Chicago. The Institute of Positive Education (IPE) was still going strong when this book went to press, and the connectedness and fortitude of the Black institution builders who granted me interviews— Dr. Safisha Madhubuti (Carol D. Lee), Dr. Haki Madhubuti, Dr. Jabari Mahiri, Dr. Kimya Moyo, and Mrs. Soyini Walton—was a reminder collective work bears fruit as more power and new possibilities. Thank you all for trusting me with your stories and your time. I'm additionally grateful to Third World Press Foundation, especially Ms. Rose, an incredible source of support. The Madhubutis, ever generous, made sure I could spend time at Third World Press and the Betty Shabazz International Charter Schools. Thank you, Baba Shannon (Sundiata) Mason and Mama Nakia Thurmond, and all the incredible educators I had the honor of spending time with at IPE schools.

Dr. Yaoundé Olu's art and editorial cartoons, featured throughout the pages of IPE's *Black Books Bulletin* literary journal, and K. Kofi Moyo's photographic documentation of IPE have been additional sources of inspiration. I am grateful to and for both of them.

My time as an Andrew W. Mellon Foundation Fellow at the Center for Advanced Study in the Behavioral Sciences (CASBS) at Stanford University during the 2022/23 academic year was instrumental to the development of this book manuscript. I'm especially indebted to Jean Beaman, Adam Goodman, and Woody Powell for taking time to engage my work. Other fellows and visiting scholars took interest and also offered helpful feedback, including Riana Elyse Anderson, Simukai Chigudu, Nitsan Chirov, Hannah Eagleson, Kuukuwa Manful, Nathan Matias, Sylvia Perry, Dianne Pinderhughes, Rohini Somanathan, and Martin Williams. Also amazing members of the CASBS community were librarians Jason Gonzalez and Fatma Massoud, who played critical roles during my fellowship. Where would any of us be without librarians and special collections? Victor Collymore-Bey and Barrye Brown at the Schomburg Center for Research in Black Culture were phenomenal, as were the teams at Special Collections Stanford Libraries and Christine Cheng of UC Davis Archives and Special Collections.

Many colleagues have supported me throughout this writing process. I'm especially grateful to and for Bianca Baldridge, Orly Clerge, Darnel Degand, John Diamond, Jarvis Givens, Jennifer Higgs, Michael Hines, Robin D. G. Kelley, Lorena Marquez, Alexis Patterson, John and Angela Rickford, Vanessa Siddle-Walker, Elizabeth Todd-Breland, and Nim Tottenham. Colleagues in Stanford University's Graduate School of Education and Stanford Accelerator for Learning have been invaluable, helping me think about this work in even more expansive ways. This has also been the case with my Futuring for Equity Lab team. I can never forget my foundation—the Transformative Justice in Education Center at UC Davis—Lawrence "Torry" Winn, Andre Anderson-Thompson, Carrissah Calvin, Ambar Hernandez, Adam Musser, Misbah Naseer, Izamar Ortiz-Gonzalez, and Vanessa Segundo. Lisa Wong Jackson and Tawnya Fay Switzer always have my back; I'm beyond grateful to both for their creativity and vision, as well as how they support me in articulating mine.

There are no words for the endless love and generosity of my husband, Torry, and our sons, Obasi and Zafir.

Notes

Foreword

1. In addition to serving as associate editor of Hoyt W. Fuller's journal *The Black World*, Carole A. Parks was an early member of the Organization of Black American Culture and later co-edited *Nommo: A Literary Legacy of Black Chicago, 1967–1987* (Chicago: Obahouse, 1987). See also Haki R. Madhubuti and Lasana D. Kazembe [interview], "A New Music Screaming in the Sun: Haki R. Madhubuti and the Nationalization/Internationalization of Chicago's BAM," *Chicago Review* 62, no. 4 (2019): 110.
2. Carole A. Parks, "Goodbye Black Sambo: Black Writers Forge New Images in Children's Literature," *Ebony* 28, no. 1 (November 1972): 60–62, 67–70.
3. Melissa Barton, "Guide to the Joseph W. Rollins, Sr. and Charlemae Rollins Collection, 1897–1989," (2005), https://mts.lib.uchicago.edu/collections/findingaids/index.php?eadid=MTS.rollins; "Charlemae Hill Rollins Papers," https://www.chipublib.org/fa-charlemae-hill-rollins-papers; Anne Meis Knupfer, *The Chicago Black Renaissance and Women's Activism* (Urbana: University of Illinois Press, 2006), 61–63; Cass Mabbott, "The We Need Diverse Books Campaign and Critical Race Theory: Charlemae Rollins and the Call for Diverse Children's Books," *Library Trends* 65, no. 4 (2017): 515–516; "Transcript: Library for the People Episode 2: The Library as the Soul of the Community," Library For the People podcast, June 15, 2023, https://www.chipublib.org/transcript-library-for-the-people-episode-2. Rollins's books include *Christmas Gif': An Anthology of Christmas Poems, Songs and Stories Written by and about Negroes* (New York: Follett Publishing, 1963); *They Showed the Way: Forty American Negro Leaders* (New York: Thomas Y. Crowell, 1964); *Famous American Negro Poets* (New York: Dodd, Mead, 1965); *Famous Negro Entertainers of Stage, Screen and TV* (New York: Dodd, Mead, 1967); and *Black Troubadour Langston Hughes* (Chicago: Rand McNally, 1970).
4. George E. Lewis, *A Power Stronger than Itself: The AACM and American Experimental Music* (London: University of Chicago Press, 2008), 179.
5. One of the most popular books among Black militants at the time was Sidney Willhelm's *Who Needs the Negro?* (Cambridge, MA: Schenkman

NOTES TO PAGES 1–4

Publishing, 1970). Its title was more ominous than the actual argument, which predicted that automation would lead to permanent unemployment for African Americans.

Introduction

1. K. Kofi Moyo captured many images of the work of IPE. Moyo's photos are in Haki Madhubuti's book *From Plan to Planet*, and appear throughout *Black Books Bulletin* journal issues, the full run of which is held in the Shule Jumamose Archive.
2. Poets Carolyn Rodgers and Johari Amini provided early support to Third World Press.
3. The cover and contents of *Imani* 5, no. 2 (1971), published by the Black Allied Student Association at New York University, was dedicated to the "rise of Independent Black Educational Institutions" and contained several essays examining the efforts of Black institution builders throughout the United States.
4. Some IPE visionaries said the council was "Baraza ya Kati" and others said it was "Baraza ya Kazi." *Kazi* was a popular term (Kiswahili for "work") that signaled the work ethic of Black institution builders. There were songs and chants of "Kazi is the Blackest of them all," and some documents in the Shule Jumamose Archive close with this affirmation, as well. See Carol D. Lee, "Profile of an Independent Black Institution: African-Centered Education at Work," *Journal of Negro History* 61, no. 2 (1992): 161.
5. Lee, "Profile of an Independent," 161.
6. I interviewed Soyini Walton on March 22, 2022, via Zoom.
7. Scholars often reference 1965 as the beginning of the Black Arts Movement. This coincides with the assassination of Malcolm X, the poet LeRoi Jones's transformation to Amiri Baraka, and the establishment of the Black Arts Repertory Theatre/School (BART/S) in Harlem, which has often been viewed as the institutional origin of the Black Arts Movement. See La Donna L. Forsgren, *Sistuhs in the Struggle: An Oral History of Black Arts Movement Theater and Performance* (Evanston, IL: Northwestern University Press, 2020); La Donna L. Forsgren, *In Search of Our Warrior Mothers: Women Dramatists of the Black Arts Movement* (Evanston, IL: Northwestern University Press, 2018). Whereas Forsgren uses 1965 to late 1970s periodization for the Black Arts Movement, for scholarship that uses 1965 to 1975, see James Edward Smethurst, *The Black Arts Movement: Literary Nationalism in the 1960s and 1970s* (Chapel Hill: University of North Carolina Press, 2005).
8. Institute for the Future was founded in 1968 as a nonprofit specializing in supporting communities of practice in acquiring skills and tools to become future-ready.

9. The COVID-19 global pandemic exacerbated inequalities across domains and in education, and I recognize my own privilege as a professional who was able to work comfortably from home during the height of the pandemic.

10. See Associated Press, "'We Feel Safer': Black Parents Say Remote Learning Gives Kids Reprieve from Racism," *Today*, May 6, 2021, www.today.com/parents/we-feel-safer-black-parents-say-remote-learning-gives-kids-t217696; Pia Ceres, "They Rage-Quit the School System—and They're Not Going Back," *Wired*, June 3, 2021, www.wired.com/story/pandemic-homeschoolers-who-are-not-going-back; Moriah Balingit and Kate Rabinowitz, "Homeschooling Exploded Among Black, Asian, and Latino Students. But It Wasn't Just the Pandemic," *Washington Post*, July 27, 2021, www.washingtonpost.com/education/2021/07/27/pandemic-homeschool-black-asian-hispanic-families. Scholar Cheryl Fields-Smith, long at the forefront of research on Black family homeschool educators, established a portal for parent educators and scholars, Black Family Homeschool Educators and Scholars (BFHES), https://blackfamilyhomeschool.com.

11. Haki R. Madhubuti, *From Plan to Planet Life Studies: The Need for Afrikan Minds and Institutions* (Chicago: Third World Press, 1973).

12. In February 2023, Haki Madhubuti invited me to write an essay to serve as an introduction to a reissue of *Plan to Planet*.

13. *Shule* is Kiswahili for school. *Jumamosi* is Kiswahili for Saturday. Founders changed the spelling to Jumamose.

14. Black United Fund of Sacramento Valley Inc. African American Nonprofit Leadership, "The Sacramento Kwanzaa Story: Past & Present," *Hands Together!* 1, no. 2 (Fall/Winter 2006–2007), Shule Jumamose Archive, Sacramento, CA (hereafter, Shule Jumamose Archive).

15. As I started to conceptualize this project, one of my mentors, historian Vanessa Siddle Walker, told me to interview my father immediately; in her words, "the archive is here and you need to put him in conversation with it." I did then conduct a series of interviews with my father, Dr. James Adolphus Fisher. This excerpt is from a session that took place in Sacramento, California, on June 20, 2019.

16. On the bottom right corner of the "All Learning" statement in the Shule Jumamose Archive is a citation: "El Hajj Malik Shabazz School, 630 Gough, San Francisco." Shule Jumamose Archive.

17. African American homeschooling is not new and has been written about by both scholars and homeschoolers themselves. See Grace Llewellyn, *Freedom Challenge: African American Homeschoolers* (Eugene, OR: Lowry House Publishing, 1996); Paula Penn-Nabrit, *Morning by Morning: How We Home-Schooled Our African-American Sons to the Ivy League* (New York: Villard, 2003).

132 · NOTES TO PAGES 10–13

18. Many futurists frame their work as an effort to arrive to the future early. Here, I am playing on the title of Bob Johansen's *Get There Early: Sending the Future to Compete in the Present* (Oakland, CA: Berrett-Koehler Publishers, 2007).

19. Rebecca Zorach, *Art for People's Sake: Artists and Community in Black Chicago, 1965–1975* (Durham, NC: Duke University Press, 2019), 7.

20. Imani Perry, *Looking for Lorraine: The Radiant and Radical Life of Lorraine Hansberry* (Boston: Beacon Press, 2018), 17–18.

21. René de Guzman, "A Question of Memory: A Conversation with Angela Y. Davis," recorded in October 2019 and featured in the Oakland Museum of California's *Angela Davis: Seize the Time* exhibition (October 2022–June 2023). Transcript available online through the Goethe-Institut, April 2021, https://www.goethe.de/ins/us/en/kul/art/one/22172673.html.

22. Interview with James A. Fisher, Sacramento, California, June 20, 2019.

23. Angela Ards, "Haki Madhubuti: The Measure of a Man," *Black Issues Book Review*, March–April 2002, 43. Third World Press celebrated its fifty-fifth anniversary in 2022, and the New Concept School became a full-time preschool in 1974, after launching initially as a Saturday School. IPE also houses the Betty Shabazz International Charter Schools—Betty Shabazz Academy and Barbara Sizemore Academy—which do not fall under the umbrella of "independent." IPE was criticized by the Council of Independent Black Institutions and other Black cultural nationalists for this move; see Worth Kamili Hayes, *Schools of Our Own: Chicago's Golden Age of Black Private Education* (Evanston, IL: Northwestern University Press, 2020).

24. James D. Anderson, *The Education of Black in the South, 1860–1935* (Chapel Hill: University of North Carolina Press, 1988), 6.

25. Haki R. Madhubuti, "Foreword. Cultural Work: Planting New Trees with New Seeds," in *Too Much Schooling, Too Little Education: A Paradox of Black Life in White Societies*, ed. Mwalimu J. Shujaa (Trenton, NJ: African World Press, 1994), 4.

26. Shujaa, "Introduction to Part Four," in Shujaa, ed., *Too Much Schooling*, 267.

27. This is part of the *Black Books Bulletin* mission statement included on the inside cover of the inaugural 1971 issue and in subsequent issues.

28. Vanessa Siddle Walker, *Their Highest Potential* (Chapel Hill: University of North Carolina Press, 1996).

29. Maree Conway, "Defining Futures Thinking," Foresight in the Present, Substack, May 28, 2022, https://foresightpresent.substack.com/p/defining-futures-thinking.

30. N. K. Jemison, introduction to *How Long 'til Black Future Month?* (New York: Orbit Books, 2018), x. "How Long 'til Black Future Month?: The Toxins of Speculative Fiction and the Antidote That Is Janelle Monae" was first published on Jemisin's blog, nkjemisin.com, on September 30, 2013, though the post is no longer available.

31. Interview with Haki Madhubuti, January 25, 2022, via Zoom.

32. Maisha T. Winn, "Futures Matter: Creating Just Futures in This Age of Hyper-incarceration," *Peabody Journal of Education* 96, no. 5 (2021), 527–539; Maisha T. Winn, "Imagining Equity: Leveraging the 5 Pedagogical Stances" (Scottsdale, AZ: Imagine Learning, 2021); Maisha T. Winn, "Paradigm Shifting Toward Justice in Teacher Education" (University of Michigan, TeachingWorks Working Paper, 2019).

33. Institute for the Future describes its foresight training as offering tools to "foster mindsets and skills that enable individuals and organizations to foresee future forces, identify emerging needs, and develop future-ready strategies." "Unleash the Power of Futures Thinking," Institute for the Future, accessed May 13, 2025, https://www.iftf.org/foresightessentials.

34. Dr. Yaoundé Olu, who created art for *Black Books Bulletin*, describes her work as retrofuturism—the ability to imagine something else while existing on the same plane as others, neither in the past nor in the future, but a meeting of both in a new space or third space. Interview, February 25, 2022 via Zoom. Robin D. G. Kelley, "Culture@Large: On Culture and Imagination," presentation at the American Anthropological Association Annual Meeting, San Jose, CA, 2018.

35. Brandon R. Byrd, Leslie M. Alexander, and Russell Rickford, eds., *Ideas in Unexpected Places: Reimagining Black Intellectual History* (Evanston, IL: Northwestern University Press, 2022). I first heard the term *citizen archivists* on August 6, 2020, from University of Notre Dame Head of University Archives Angela Fritz, who shared with me her vision that students be engaged in telling the story of the university. We were working with the Klau Center for Civil and Human Rights on the "With Voices True" project, which involved collection and curation of undergraduate students' stories about race on campus.

36. Byrd, Alexander, and Rickford, *Ideas in Unexpected Places*; Elizabeth McHenry, *Forgotten Readers: Recovering the Lost History of African American Literary Societies* (Durham, NC: Duke University Press, 2002); Elizabeth McHenry and Shirley Brice Heath, "The Literate and the Literary: African Americans as Writers and Readers 1830–1940," *Written Communication* 11, no. 4 (1994): 419–44. I extended McHenry and Brice Heath's work from 1940 through the Black Arts Movement to center the rise of spoken word poetry in the early 2000s; see Maisha T. Fisher, "The Song Is Unfinished: The New Literate and Literary and Their Institutions," *Written Communication* 21, no. 3 (2004): 290–312 (Fisher was my surname before marriage).

37. On April 11 and 12, 2023, Bianca J. Baldridge, Jarvis R. Givens, and kihana m. ross hosted "The Clearing: A Convening on Black Education Studies," with the theme "Reimagining Scholarship and Practice as the Intersection of Black Studies and Education Research" at Northwestern University in Evanston, Illinois.

34 · NOTES TO PAGES 16–24

38. kihana miraya ross and Jarvis R. Givens, "The Clearing: On Black Education Studies and the Problem of Antiblackness" *Harvard Educational Review* 93, no. 2 (2023): 149–72.

39. Jarvis R. Givens, *Fugitive Pedagogy: Carter G. Woodson and the Art of Black Teaching* (Cambridge, MA: Harvard University Press, 2021), 29.

40. I interviewed Jitu Weusi (Les Campbell) on April 24, 2007, for Maisha T. Fisher, *Black Literate Lives: Historical and Contemporary Perspectives* (New York: Routledge, 2009); this quote appears in chapter 3 as part of my discussion of Pan-Africanism and IBIs. Weusi and other Black institution builders had relationships with African leaders and sought out Julius Nyerere's teaching on African socialism, with particular attention to his Ujamaa policy values around familyhood and communal values.

41. For scholarship that centers the work of women in the Black Arts Movement, see Forsgren, *Sistuhs in the Struggle*; Forsgren, *In Search of Our Warrior Mothers*; and Lisa Gail Collins and Margo Natalie Crawford, eds., *New Thoughts on the Black Arts Movement* (New Brunswick, NJ: Rutgers University Press, 2008).

42. Carol D. Lee refers to Johari Amini-Hudson as IPE's "cultural mother." Dr. Amini-Hudson was a poet who eventually left IPE to pursue her desire to become a chiropractor. She passed away on December 12, 2023. Third World Press celebrated her life and contributions in a memorial service on January 6, 2024.

Chapter 1

1. Though I reached out to His Eminence Wilton Cardinal Gregory, who is now in Washington, DC, to learn his perspective on these happenings and Haki Madhubuti, staff said he was unavailable.

2. Conversation with Haki Madhubuti, April 21, 2023.

3. Interview with Soyini Walton, March 22, 2022, via Zoom.

4. Interview with Haki Madhubuti, January 25, 2022, via Zoom.

5. St. Clair Drake and Horace R. Cayton, *The Black Metropolis: A Study of Negro Life in a Northern City* (Harper & Row, 1945; University of Chicago Press, 2015), 398. Citations refer to the University of Chicago Press edition.

6. Ethan Michaeli, *The Defender: How the Legendary Black Newspaper Changed America* (New York: Houghton Mifflin Harcourt, 2016), 37.

7. Smethurst, *The Black Arts Movement*, 9. Smethurst notes that while he cites Kalamu ya Salaam's work, Salaam's *The Magic of Juju: An Appreciation of the Black Arts Movement* was still unpublished when *The Black Arts Movement* went to press. *The Magic of Juju* was published in 2016—by Madhubuti's Third World Press.

8. For more on Black print culture, including a historical overview, see V. P. Franklin, "To Be Heard in Black and White: Historical Perspectives on Black Print Culture," *Journal of African American History* 95, nos. 3 and 4 (Summer/

NOTES TO PAGES 25–30 · 135

Fall Special Issue, 2010); other articles in that same special issue also engage this topic.

9. "Ahidiana: An Archive of a New Orleans Pan African Nationalist Organization (1973–1988)," Ahidiana, 2021, https://www.ahidiana.com/ahidiana.

10. Merriam-Webster, "Institution," accessed May 14, 2025, https://www.merriam-webster.com/dictionary/institution.

11. Carol D. Lee, "Profile of an Independent Black Institution: African-Centered Education at Work," *Journal of Negro Education* 61, no. 2 (1992): 161.

12. Lee, "Profile," 161.

13. See McHenry, *Forgotten Readers*; Keith Gilyard, *Let's Flip the Script: An African American Discourse on Language, Literature, and Learning* (Detroit, MI: Wayne State University Press, 1996); Thomas Holt, "Knowledge Is Power: The Black Struggle for Literacy," in *The Right to Literacy*, ed. Andrea A. Lunsford, Helene Moglen, and James Slevin (New York: Modern Language Association of America).

14. Maisha T. Fisher, "Choosing Literacy: African Diaspora Participatory Literacy Communities," PhD diss., University of California at Berkeley, 2003.

15. Dianne Pinderhughes, *Race and Ethnicity in Chicago Politics: A Reexamination of Pluralist Theory* (Urbana: University of Illinois Press, 1987).

16. Komozi Woodard, *A Nation Within a Nation: Amiri Baraka (LeRoi Jones) and Black Power Politics* (Chapel Hill: University of North Carolina Press, 1999).

17. William Sites, *Sun Ra's Chicago: Afrofuturism and the City* (Chicago: University of Chicago Press, 2020), 3.

18. Sites, *Sun Ra's Chicago*, 10.

19. Marcus Anthony Hunter and Zandria F. Robinson, *Chocolate Cities: The Black Map of American Life* (Oakland: University of California Press, 2018), xiii and 5.

20. Lee, "Profile," 161.

21. Interview with Carol D. Lee, March 10, 2022, via Zoom.

22. Interview with Carol D. Lee, March 10, 2022, via Zoom

23. Zorach, *Art for People's Sake*, 10.

24. Jeff Donaldson co-founded AfriCOBRA with Wadsworth Jarrell, Barbara Jones-Hogu, and others. Murry De Pillars was an AfriCOBRA member and later Dean of Arts at Virginia Commonwealth University.

25. See Wadsworth A. Jarrell, *AFRICOBRA: Experimental Art Toward a School of Thought* (Durham, NC: Duke University Press, 2020); Zorach, *Art for People's Sake*.

26. Interview with Haki Madhubuti, January 25, 2022, via Zoom.

27. Interview with Kimya Moyo, March 21, 2022, via Zoom.

28. Madhubuti, *From Plan to Planet*. Madhubuti first published this text with Dudley Randall's Broadside Press in 1973.

29. Woodard, *Nation Within*, 75.

30. Woodard, *Nation Within*, 89.

NOTES TO PAGES 30–34

31. Ashley D. Farmer, *Remaking Black Power: How Black Women Transformed an Era* (Chapel Hill: University of North Carolina Press, 2017), 107.

32. Madhubuti, *From Plan to Planet*, 46. Worth Kamili Hayes also refers to Amiri Baraka as Karenga's "star pupil" for his study and expansion of the Nguzo Saba beyond Kwanzaa celebration—as a "Black Value System"; see Hayes, *Schools of Our Own*, 89.

33. Frank Satterwhite, ed., *Planning an Independent Black Educational Institution* (Harlem, NY: Moja Publishing House, 1971), 5. Education and Black Students was one of eleven workshop topics at the 1970 CAP convening, per the *Planning* document; the others were Political Liberation, Economic Autonomy, Creativity and the Arts, Religious Systems, History, Law and Justice, Black Technology, Communications and Systems Analysis, Social Organization, and Community Organization.

34. Woodard, *Nation Within*, 164.

35. Preston Wilcox, *Congress of African People, Council Education, Report on Education and Black Students, Atlanta, GA, Sept 1970*, box 8, file 1, CAP 1970–1972, Preston Wilcox Papers, Schomburg Center for Research on Black Culture, New York Public Library, New York.

36. Satterwhite, *Planning*, 14. Workshops at CAP's 1971 convening included "Black Studies Program Consortium," "Black Student Unions on White Campuses," "Black Teachers and Administrators in Public Schools," "Community Control of Schools," "Independent Black Educational Institutions," "Black Colleges as Employment Vehicles," "Early Childhood Development—Materials Development," "A Federal Funding Apparatus," "Language of Humanism Directory," and "Education in Confined Settings." Emphasis in original.

37. Carter G. Woodson, *Mis-education of the Negro* (Washington, DC: Associated Publishers, 1933), 2.

38. Satterwhite, *Planning*, 13.

39. Satterwhite, *Planning*, 13. Satterwhite also includes Preston Wilcox's introductory remarks for the Education and Black Students Workshop at the 1970 Congress of African People convening in Atlanta.

40. Satterwhite, *Planning*, 13.

41. Kwasi Konadu, *A View from The East: Black Cultural Nationalism and Education in New York City* (New York: Diasporic Africa Press, 2018), xx.

42. The East, *Outline for a New African Educational Institution: The Uhuru Sasa Shule School Program* (Brooklyn, NY: Black Nation Education Series #7), front matter. Shule Jumamose Archive.

43. The East, *Outline.*

44. The East, *Outline*, 3.

45. Fisher, *Black Literate Lives.*

46. Fisher, *Black Literate Lives.*

NOTES TO PAGES 35–41 · 137

47. The East, *Outline*, 11.
48. Kasisi Jitu Weusi, "From Relevance to Excellence: The Challenge of Independent Black Educational Institutions," *Black Books Bulletin* 2, nos. 3 and 4 (Winter 1974): 21.
49. Weusi, "From Relevance to Excellence," 8.
50. Mtumishi St. Julien, *Operating Principles*, Ahidiana, 1973, https://www.ahidiana.com/_files/ugd/10ecaa_ea3a92149f05414088e9f49d1f7f3cb3.pdf.
51. St. Julien, *Operating Principles*, 3.
52. St. Julien, *Operating Principles*, 3.
53. St. Julien, *Operating Principles*, 8.
54. Tayari kwa Salaam, "Practice the Values and Love Revolution," *Black Books Bulletin* 2, nos. 3 and 4 (Winter 1974): 49.
55. Salaam, "Practice the Values," 14.
56. *Black Books Bulletin* 2, nos. 3 and 4 (Winter 1974): inside back cover.

Chapter 2

1. I interviewed Jabari Mahiri on January 28, 2022, and February 25, 2022, via Zoom.
2. I am using definitions offered by the Institute for the Future.
3. Many poets, artists, parents, and community people were involved with launching the Institute of Positive Education. One visionary I was unable to interview but who was critical to IPE's development is Johari Amini (née Jewell Lattimore). Amini provided Haki Madhubuti with support in launching Third World Press and *Black Books Bulletin*. Her work was published by Third World Press. The visionaries I interviewed spoke of Amini as not only a contributor to IPE but also a tireless supporter of the overall health and wellness of everyone who worked with IPE. For Carol D. Lee's mention of IPE's "founding" group consisting of poets, including Haki Madhubuti, Johari Amini, and Sterling Plumpp, as well as educators, including herself, Jabari Mahiri, and Soyini Ricks Walton, see Lee, "Profile."
4. My interviews with IPE visionaries took place between January and March 2022 via Zoom. I met with Haki Madhubuti and Carol D. Lee in July 2022 in Martha's Vineyard, Massachusetts, where Madhubuti was a featured poet for an event celebrating the life of poet Della Hardman, and again in Chicago in April 2023 with Jabari Mahiri to continue to discuss their work. Pedagogical portraits of women actors, playwrights, and directors who taught playwriting and performance to incarcerated and formerly incarcerated girls are a centerpiece of Maisha T. Winn, *Girl Time: Literacy, Justice, and the School-to-Prison Pipeline* (New York: Teachers College Press, 2011), demonstrating what these educators brought to their shared community as individuals, and how their

138 · NOTES TO PAGES 42–47

different lived experiences, stances, and approaches to the work offered incarcerated and formerly incarcerated girls more nuanced ways to be human and think about their identities as student artists.

5. For scholarship examining the role of women in the Black Power and Black Arts movements and offering more expansive visions of institution building, see Cheryl Clarke, *"After Mecca": Women Poets and the Black Arts Movement* (New Brunswick, NJ: Rutgers University Press, 2004); and Farmer, *Remaking Black Power.*

6. Johnathan Fenderson, *Building the Black Arts Movement: Hoyt Fuller and the Cultural Politics of the 1960s* (Champaign: University of Illinois Press, 2019), 56. James Smethurst asserts that a "continuing, bidirectional interplay" endured between the national Black Arts Movement and more local initiatives; see Smethurst, *The Black Arts Movement,* 9.

7. Brent Hayes Edwards, *Epistrophies: Jazz and the Literary Imagination* (Cambridge, MA: Harvard University Press, 2017), 4.

8. Teacher, poet, and youth worker Joseph Ubiles and I provide a theoretical framework for the role researchers can and must play in self-determined communities where art is being created. I write extensively about Joseph, "Papa Joe," in Maisha T. Fisher, *Writing in Rhythm: Spoken Word Poetry in Urban Classrooms* (New York: Teachers College Press, 2007). Joseph declared my role and responsibility in his youth poetry class as being a "worthy witness," a concept we explored in a co-authored chapter, Maisha T. Winn and Joseph Ubiles, "Worthy Witnessing: Collaborative Research in Urban Classrooms," in *Studying Diversity in Teacher Education,* ed. Arnetha Ball and Cynthia Tyson (Lanham, MD: Rowman & Littlefield, 2011). I explore the concept further in Django Paris and Maisha T. Winn, *Humanizing Research: Decolonizing Qualitative Research with Communities* (Thousand Oaks, CA: Sage Publishing, 2014).

9. Interview with Haki Madhubuti, January 25, 2022, via Zoom.

10. Richard Wright, *White Man, Listen!* (Garden City, NY: Doubleday, 1957), 145.

11. Madhubuti talked about the definition of "Blackness" according to Malauna Karenga, who introduced the pillars of color, culture, and consciousness in the Seven Principles of Blackness, also known as the Nguzo Saba or Kwanzaa.

12. See Haki R. Madhubuti, "The Latest Purge: The Attack on Black Nationalism and Pan-Afrikanism by the New Left, the Sons and Daughters of the Old Left," *The Black Scholar* 6, no. 1 (September 1974): 43–56. For a rebuttal by a co-founder of Ahidiana Work/Study Center, and IBI in New Orleans, see Kalamu ya Salaam, "A Response to Haki Madhubuti," *The Black Scholar* 6, no. 5 (1975): 40–53.

13. Madhubuti, *From Plan to Planet,* 31.

14. Russell Rickford, *We Are an African People: Independent Education, Black Power, and the Radical Imagination* (Oxford: Oxford University Press, 2016). Rickford's is by far the most comprehensive study of Independent Black Educational

Institutions and should be referenced for macro-level understanding of these schools. I have written extensively about the Uhuru Sasa school that was a part of The East organization in Brooklyn; see Fisher, *Black Literate Lives*. See also Konadu, *A View from The East*.

15. Interview with Carol D. Lee, March 10, 2022, via Zoom.

16. Hanibal Afrik, formerly Harold E. Charles, established Shule Ya Watoto in 1972; it remained open for thirty-one years. Shule Ya Watoto translates to "School for Children."

17. Carol D. Lee has published many articles and a book examining cultural modeling. For example, see Carol D. Lee, *Culture, Literacy, and Learning: Taking Bloom in the Midst of a Whirlwind* (New York: Teachers College Press, 2007).

18. Jakobi Williams, *From the Bullet to the Ballot: The Illinois Chapter of The Black Panther Party and Racial Coalition Politics in Chicago* (Chapel Hill: University of North Carolina Press, 2013), 16.

19. Williams, *From the Bullet*, 18.

20. The Egyptian principles of Maat, or Ma'at, include Truth, Justice, Harmony, Balance, Order, Reciprocity, and Propriety.

21. Interview with Soyini Walton, March 22, 2023, via Zoom.

22. Sonia Sanchez shared "Catch the Fire" in a reading/keynote at the 1994 Furious Flower Conference; it is included in her anthology Sonia Sanchez, *Wounded in the House of a Friend* (Boston: Beacon Press, 1995).

23. Elizabeth Todd-Breland, *A Political Education: Black Politics and Education Reform in Chicago since the 1960s* (Chapel Hill: University of North Carolina Press, 2018), 81.

24. Todd-Breland, *A Political Education*, 109.

25. "Draft Agreement Between Afro-American Student Union and FMO and a Committee Representing the Northwestern University Administration," Northwestern University, May 4, 1968, https://sites.northwestern.edu/bursars1968.

26. Northwestern University's dedicated online exhibit "They Demanded Courageously: The 1968 Bursar's Office Take Over" documents the May 4th Agreement and includes stories, photos, primary source documents, and a documentary; see https://www.northwestern.edu/bursars-takeover/index.html.

27. See Fisher, *Black Literate Lives*.

28. Elsewhere, I examine the role of Black bookstores in cultivating a "new literate and literary." See Maisha T. Fisher, "'The Song Is Unfinished': The New Literate and Literary and their Institutions," *Written Communication* 21, no. 3 (2004): 290–312; Maisha T. Fisher, "Earning Dual Degrees: Black Bookstores as Alternative Knowledge Spaces," *Anthropology and Education Quarterly* 37, no. 1 (2006): 83–99; and Maisha T. Fisher, "'Every City Has Soldiers': The Role of Intergenerational Relationships in Participatory Literacy Communities," *Research in the Teaching of English* 42, no. 2 (2007): 139–62.

140 · NOTES TO PAGES 63–77

Chapter 3

1. Interview with Dr. Yaoundé Olu, February 2022, via Zoom. During the interview, she and I looked at the cover art she had created for the Summer 1976 issue of *Black Books Bulletin*. Dr. Olu talked about Haki Madhubuti's vision for the issue and cover, as well as her own practice of retrofuturism in her work.
2. Interview with Soyini Walton in February 2022, via Zoom.
3. "BBB Interviews Malauna Karenga," *Black Books Bulletin* 4, no. 2 (Summer 1976): 33.
4. "BBB Interviews Malauna Karenga," 32–39.
5. Fisher, *Black Literate Lives*.
6. *The Black Collegian* started in 1970 and moved online in November 1995.
7. *Unity and Struggle* was initially published as *Black NewArk* in April 1968. When the Committee for Unified Newark transformed itself into the Congress of African People, in 1974, the newspaper changed its name, as well.
8. Interview with Jabari Mahiri, January 28, 2022 via Zoom.
9. Interview with Kimya Moyo, March 21, 2022 via Zoom.
10. Interview with Jabari Mahiri, January 28, 2022 via Zoom.
11. Fisher, "Choosing Literacy"; Fisher, *Black Literate Lives*.
12. Interview with Jabari Mahiri, January 28, 2022 via Zoom.
13. Interview with Jabari Mahiri, January 28, 2022 via Zoom. The Association for the Advancement of Creative Musicians was established in 1964 in Chicago and continues to support collaborative work between and among musicians today.
14. An advertisement for IPE, published on the inside back cover of the Winter 1974 issue of *Black Books Bulletin*, outlined all IPE entities and situated IPE as a "resource-research community center."
15. IPE advertisement in Winter 1974 issue of *Black Books Bulletin*.
16. Haki Madhubuti was still publishing under the name Don L. Lee at the time this essay was published.
17. Don L. Lee, "What We Are About," *Black Books Bulletin* 1, no. 1 (1971): 25.
18. Lee, "What We Are About."
19. Lee, "What We Are About."
20. This phrasing comes from my second interview with Jabari Mahiri, in February 2022.
21. Jabari Mahiri, interview, February 2022.
22. Jabari Mahiri, interview, February 2022.
23. When Barbara Sizemore passed away, Carol D. Lee wrote a tribute. Carol D. Lee, "Remembering Barbara Ann Sizemore 1927–2004," *Educational Researcher* 33, no. 8 (November 2004).
24. "BBB Interviews Barbara Sizemore," *Black Books Bulletin* 2, nos. 3 and 4 (Winter 1974): 58.
25. "BBB Interviews Barbara Sizemore," 58.

NOTES TO PAGES 77–84 · 141

26. Regarding the Black Power Movement as part and parcel of the Civil Rights Movement, see Peniel Joseph, *Waiting 'til the Midnight Hour: A Narrative History of the Black Power Movement* (New York: Macmillan Publishers, 2007); Peniel Joseph, ed., *The Black Power Movement: Rethinking the Civil Rights/Black Power Era* (London: Routledge, 2006).

27. Rickford, *We Are an African People*, 128.

28. Amiri Baraka, *Kawaida Studies: The New Nationalism* (Chicago, IL: Third World Press, 1972) is a collection of essays that attempt to unpack Karenga's Nguzo Saba.

29. "BBB Interviews Amiri Baraka," *Black Books Bulletin* 2, no. 2 (Fall 1974): 35.

30. "BBB Interviews Malauna Ron Karenga," *Black Books Bulletin* 4, no. 2 (Summer 1976): 34.

31. "BBB Interviews Malauna Ron Karenga," 34.

32. "BBB Interviews Malauna Ron Karenga," 38.

33. "BBB Interviews Hoyt Fuller," *Black Books Bulletin* 1, no. 1 (Fall 1971): 23.

34. Fenderson, *Building the Black Arts Movement*, 2.

35. Fenderson, *Building the Black Arts Movement*, 6–7.

36. Haki R. Madhubuti, "*Black World*: The Silencing of a Giant," *Black Books Bulletin* 4, no. 2 (Summer 1976): 11.

37. "BBB Interviews Maulana Ron Karenga," *Black Books Bulletin* 4, no. 2 (Summer 1976): 32–39.

38. "BBB Interviews Gwendolyn Brooks," *Black Books Bulletin* 2, no. 1 (1974): 34.

39. Interview with Kimya Moyo

40. Interview with Kimya Moyo, March 21, 2022, via Zoom.

41. Russell Rickford, "Kazi Is the Blackest of All: Pan-African Nationalism and the Making of the 'New Man': 1969–1975," *Journal of African American History* 101, nos. 1–2 (Winter–Spring 2016): 99.

42. Interview with Kimya Moyo, March 21, 2022, via Zoom.

43. "President Gerald R. Ford's Address Before a Joint Session of the Congress Reporting on the State of the Union," Gerald Ford Presidential Library & Museum, January 15, 1975, https://www.fordlibrarymuseum.gov/library/speeches/750028.asp.

44. *Black Books Bulletin* 3, no. 2 (Summer 1975): 29.

45. George Salter, "Spinal Manipulations: A Key to Health," *Black Books Bulletin* 3, no. 2 (Summer 1975): 4–7.

46. "Tai Chi Ch'uan, the Art of Healing," *Black Books Bulletin* 3, no. 2 (Summer 1975): 36.

47. Dolores Robinson, "High Blood Pressure (HYPERTENSION): The Most Serious Health Problem Faced by Blacks in America," *Black Books Bulletin* 3, no. 2 (Summer 1975): 14.

48. Wade Nobles, "The Black Family and Its Children: The Survival of Humaneness," *Black Books Bulletin* 6, no. 2 (1978): 8.

142 · NOTES TO PAGES 84–92

49. Both *Black Books Bulletin* 4, no. 3 (Fall 1976) and 7, no. 2 (1981) were dedicated to Black psychology; they included articles by Frances Kress-Welsing, Asa Hilliard, and Na'im Akbar.
50. "BBB interviews Dr. Na'im Akbar," *Black Books Bulletin* 4, no. 3 (Fall 1976): 35.
51. Asa G. Hilliard III, "I.Q. Thinking as Catechism: Ethnic and Cultural Bias or Invalid Science?" *Black Books Bulletin* 7, no. 2 (1981): 2.
52. Hilliard, "I.Q. Thinking," 7.
53. Amos Wilson, "The Psychological Development of the Black Child," *Black Books Bulletin* 7, no. 2 (1981): 13.
54. "BBB Interviews Amos Wilson," *Black Books Bulletin* 7, no. 2 (1981): 36.

Chapter 4

1. Gerald McDermott, *The Magic Tree: A Tale from the Congo* (New York: Holt, Rinehart, and Winston, 1973).
2. Review of *The Magic Tree*, Books for the Young, *Black Books Bulletin* 2, no. 2 (Fall 1974): 66.
3. Review of *The Magic Tree*, 66.
4. The 1970s saw a wave of children's literature that continues to capture the popular imagination, including Dr. Seuss's *The Lorax*, Arnold Lobel's *Frog and Toad Are Friends*, and Maurice Sendak's *In the Night Kitchen*, which was later banned for nudity.
5. Review of *The Magic Tree*, 66.
6. Fisher, *Black Literate Lives*, 59.
7. After Johnson Publications introduced *Ebony Jr.* in May 1973, Books for the Young gave a favorable review and declared it "the perfect magazine for Black children. Nothing is missing." See Review of *Ebony Jr.*, *Black Books Bulletin* 2, no. 1 (1974): 39.
8. Lee, "What We Are About," 25.
9. Lee, "What We Are About," 25.
10. On January 18, 1975, American television watchers were introduced to African American businessman George Jefferson and his family, who had risen to middle- and upper-class status after George's success with a dry cleaning business.
11. This quote comes from the inside back cover of the Winter 1974 issue of *Black Books Bulletin*, which focused on children and education.
12. Cedric J. Robinson, "Blaxploitation and the Misrepresentation of Liberation," *Race & Class* 40, no. 1 (1998): 1–12.
13. Yaoundé Olu, "Who Controls *Their* Images?" (cartoon), *Black Books Bulletin* 2, nos. 3 and 4 (Winter 1974): 85.
14. Francis Ward, *"Super Fly": A Political and Cultural Condemnation by the Kuumba Workshop* (Chicago, IL: Institute of Positive Education, 1972). Shule Juma-mose Archive.

NOTES TO PAGES 92–103 · 143

15. Ward, *"Super Fly,"* n.p.

16. Lee, "What We Are About," 25.

17. Madhubuti, *From Plan to Planet*, 30.

18. Madhubuti, *From Plan to Planet*, 30.

19. *Black Books Bulletin*, 2, nos. 3 and 4 (Winter 1974): 3.

20. Madhubuti, *From Plan to Planet*, 82.

21. Review of *Children of Africa*, Books for the Young, *Black Books Bulletin* 1, no. 2 (Winter 1972): 56.

22. Review of *Children of Africa*, 56.

23. Drum and Spear Press, *Children of Africa: A Coloring Book* (Washington DC: Drum and Spear Press, 1972), n.p. Shule Jumamose Archive.

24. For complementary framing, see Julius Nyerere, *UJAMAA: Essays on Socialism* (Oxford: Oxford University Press, 1974).

25. Drum and Spear Press, *Children of Africa*.

26. *Black Books Bulletin*'s mission statement was printed on the front inside cover of every issue.

27. Books for the Young, *Black Books Bulletin* 1, No. 2 (Winter 1972): 56.

28. Drum and Spear Press, *Children of Africa*, opening page.

29. Review of *Rosa Parks*, Books for the Young, *Black Books Bulletin* 2, no. 2 (Fall 1974): 65.

30. Review of *Rosa Parks*, 65.

31. Seth M. Markel, "Publishers for a Pan African World: Drum and Spear Press and Tanzania's Ujamaa Ideology," *The Black Scholar* 37, no. 4 (Winter 2008): 16–26.

32. Charlie Cobb, *African Notebook: Views on Returning Home* (Chicago, IL: Institute of Positive Education, 1972).

33. Jabari Mahiri, review of *I Want to Be*, Books for the Young, *Black Books Bulletin* 2, nos. 3 and 4 (Winter 1974): 81.

34. Mahiri, review of *I Want to Be*.

35. Christine C. Johnson, *ABCs of African History* (New York: Vantage Press, 1971).

36. Review of *ABCs of African History*, Books for the Young, *Black Books Bulletin* 1, no. 2 (Winter 1972): 54.

37. Review of *ABCs of African History*.

38. Kasisi Yusef Iman, *The Weusi Alfabeti* (Brooklyn, NY: The East, 1979).

39. Kalamu ya Salaam and Tayari kwa Salaam, *Herufi: An Alphabet Reader* (New Orleans, LA: Kuumba Na Kazi / Ahidiana Habari, 1978).

40. "Books for the Young," *Black Books Bulletin* 1, no. 1 (1971): 34.

41. "Books for the Young," 34.

42. Mary W. Sullivan, *Jokers Wild* (Boston: Addison-Wesley Educational Publishers, 1970).

43. Review of *Jokers Wild*, Books for the Young, *Black Books Bulletin* 1, no. 1 (1971): 34.

44. Josh Levin, *The Queen: The Forgotten Life Behind an American Myth* (New York: Back Bay Books, 2020).

45. Review of *Jokers Wild*, 34.

46. Review of *Teacup Full of Roses*, Books for the Young, *Black Books Bulletin* 1, no. 4 (1973): 35.

47. Janet Harris, review of "Teacup Full of Roses," *New York Times*, September 10, 1972, BR8.

48. Sharon Bell Mathis, "True/False Messages for the Black Child," *Black Books Bulletin* 2, nos. 3 and 4 (1974): 12–19.

49. Bell Mathis, "True/False Messages," 16.

50. Review of *Listen for the Fig Tree*, Books for the Young, *Black Books Bulletin* 2, no. 1 (1974): 39.

51. Review of *Listen for the Fig Tree*, 39.

52. Jane D. Shackelford, *The Child's Story of the Negro* (Washington DC: Associated Press, 1938), 101.

53. For recent related undertakings, see Karida L. Brown and Charly Palmer, *The New Brownies' Book: A Love Letter to Black Families* (San Francisco, CA: Chronicle Books, 2023); Amato Nocera, "'May We Not Write Our Own Fairy Tales and Make Black Beautiful?': African American Teachers, Children's Literature, and the Construction of Race in the Curriculum, 1920–1945," *History of Education Quarterly* 63, no. 1 (2023), examining the work of Jane Dabney Shackelford and Helen Adele Whiting; and Michael Hines, *A Worthy Piece of Work: The Untold Story of Madeline Morgan and the Fight for Black History in Schools* (Boston: Beacon Press, 2022). Nocera and Hines both highlight the work of Black women in the efforts to get Black history curricula recognized by school systems.

54. Review of *The Child's Story of the Negro*, Books for the Young, *Black Books Bulletin* 1, no. 2 (1972).

55. Review of *The Child's Story of the Negro*, 54.

56. Review of *Stevie*, Books for the Young, *Black Books Bulletin* 1, no. 1 (Fall 1971): 34.

57. Review of *Stevie*, 34.

58. Review of *Stevie*, 34.

59. "John Steptoe New Talent Award," Coretta Scott King Book Awards Round Table, American Library Association, accessed May 14, 2025, https://www.ala.org/cskbart/cskbookawards/johnsteptoe.

60. Review of *Childtimes: A Three Generational Memoir*, Books for the Young, *Black Books Bulletin* 7, no. 2 (1981): 56.

61. Hoyt W. Fuller, "Towards a Black Aesthetic," in *The Black Aesthetic*, ed. Addison Gayle Jr. (Garden City, NY: Doubleday, 1971), 16.

62. Addison Gayle Jr., ed., *The Black Aesthetic* (Garden City, NY: Doubleday, 1971), xxiii.

63. Gayle, *The Black Aesthetic*, xxiv.

64. Review of *Jackie*, Books for the Young, *Black Books Bulletin* 1, no. 1 (Fall 1971): 34.

65. See Fisher, *Black Literate Lives*.
66. Review of *The Tiger Who Wore White Gloves*, Books for the Young, *Black Books Bulletin* 2, no. 2 (Fall 1974): 63.
67. Review of *The Tiger Who Wore*, 63.
68. Review of *The Tiger Who Wore*, 63.
69. Interview with Jabari Mahiri, January 28, 2022, via Zoom.
70. Interview with Jabari Mahiri, January 28, 2022, via Zoom.
71. Sonia Sanchez, *It's a New Day: (Poems for Young Brothas and Sistuhs)* (Detroit, MI: Broadside Press, 1971).

Chapter 5

Epigraphs: Kimya Moyo, from interview on March 21, 2022; Soyini Walton, from interview on March 22, 2022.

1. Interview with Jabari Mahiri, February 25, 2022.
2. Here, I am thinking about Theresa Lillis's notion of ethnography as method, methodology, and "deep theorizing." See, for example, her examination of research on academic writing: Theresa Lillis, "Ethnography as Method, Methodology, and 'Deep Theorizing': Closing the Gap Between Text and Context in Academic Writing and Research," *Written Communication* 25, no. 3 (2008): 353–88.
3. See Siddle Walker, *Their Highest Potential*; Vanessa Siddle Walker, *Hello Professor: A Black Principal and Professional Leadership in the Segregated South* (Chapel Hill: University of North Carolina Press, 2009); Allyson Hobbs, "Black Lives Matter and the Power of Protest," posted to YouTube by Stanford University Alumni, August 4, 2020, www.youtube.com/watch?v=EebMPwRr6Hs; and Manning Marable, *Living Black History: How Reimagining the African-American Past Can Remake America's Racial Future* (New York: Basic Civitas Books, 2006).
4. Hayes, *School of Our Own*, 3.
5. Statements transcribed from our conversation on April 13, 2023, at the Fairmont Chicago Millennium, one of the conference hotels for the 2023 American Educational Research Association Annual Meeting.
6. Interview with Carol D. Lee, March 10, 2022.
7. Both Carol D. Lee and Jabari Mahiri discussed during interviews some of the commitments IPE tried to make regarding work distribution and shared leadership goals. Chapter 3 presents some of Mahiri's thoughts regarding the expectation that men nurture close relationships with children and be engaged in education programs; he acknowledged that, like other organizations rooted in the Black liberation movement, IPE did not always get this right.
8. Statements transcribed from our conversation on April 13, 2023.
9. Maitefa Angaza, "The International African Arts Festival Celebrates 50 Years of Fun in Building Unity," *Our Time Press*, accessed on May 4, 2025.

146 · NOTES TO PAGES 115–123

https://ourtimepress.com/the-international-african-arts-festival-celebrates-50-years-of-fun-in-building-unity; Amsterdam News Staff, "48th Annual African Arts Festival Marks 50th Anniversary of the Founding of the East Organization," Amsterdam News, June 6, 2019, https://amsterdamnews.com/news/2019/06/06/48th-annual-african-arts-festival-marks-50th-anniv.

10. Tayo Giwa and Cynthia Gordy Giwa, writers, *The Sun Rises in the East: The Birth, Rise, and Legacy of Brooklyn's Black Nation* (Black-Owned Brooklyn, 2022), 58 min. At the time this book went to press, this film was streaming on several platforms.

11. Quote from Dwana A. Smallwood, a former principal dancer for Alvin Ailey American Dance Theater and a Uhuru Sasa alumna who appears in the documentary.

12. Black-Owned Brooklyn, 2018, www.blackownedbrooklyn.com. At the time of this writing, Black-Owned Brooklyn's Instagram account had 119K followers.

13. Akane Okoshi, *The Sun Rises in the East: A Documentary Film by Tayo Giwa and Cynthia Gordy Giwa, Discussion and Activity Guide* (Brooklyn, NY: Black-Owned Brooklyn, 2023), www.sunrisesintheeast.com.

14. Tayari kwa Salaam, "Memories of Ahidiana," Ahidiana Remembrance, 2019, https://www.ahidiana.com/_files/ugd/10ecaa_e7389efed263404ca9e291d-670dee810.pdf.

15. In addition to New Concept preschool established in 1974, as this book goes to press IPE continues to operate Betty Shabazz Academy, a K–8 charter school opened in 1998 and named after Malcolm X's wife, Dr. Betty Shabazz, an educator in her own right, and also Barbara A. Sizemore Academy, a K–8 charter school established in 2005. Barbara Sizemore was featured in the *Bulletin*'s 1974 Special Issue on Children and Education and mentored several IPE visionaries.

16. Interview with Carol D. Lee, March 10, 2022, via Zoom.

17. Interview with Kimya Moyo, March 21, 2022, via Zoom.

18. Interview with Soyini Walton, March 22, 2022, via Zoom.

19. Interview with Haki Madhubuti, January 25, 2022, via Zoom.

Epilogue

1. Betty Shabazz International Charter School, Student and Family Handbook, Morning Unity Circle Pledge (Opening Ritual), 2021–22 academic year.

Bibliography

Special Collections

Archives and Special Collections, UC Davis Library, Davis, California.
Schomburg Center for Research in Black Culture, Manuscripts, Archives and
Rare Books Division, Preston Wilcox papers, New York City, New York.
Shule Jumamose Archive, Author's Personal Collection, Sacramento, California.
Stanford Libraries Special Collections, Stanford, California.

Oral History Interviews by Author

Fisher, James A. Audio recording. Sacramento, California. May 25, 2019;
June 20, 2019.
Lee, Carol D. Zoom recording. March 10, 2022.
Madhubuti, Haki R. Zoom recording. January 25, 2022.
Mahiri, Jabari. Zoom recording. January 28, 2022 and February 25, 2022.
Moyo, Kimya. Zoom recording. March 21, 2022.
Olu, Yaoundé. Zoom recording. February 25, 2022.
Walton, Soyini. Zoom recording. March 22, 2022.

Additional Interviews Consulted

Lee, Carol D. (Safisha Madhubuti). Interview by The History Makers, October 4,
2021, https://www.thehistorymakers.org.
Madhubuti, Haki. Interview by The History Makers, December 20, 1999 and April
14, 2002, https://www.thehistorymakers.org.
Madhubuti, Haki. "Interview with Haki R. Madhubuti of Institute of Positive
Education, Chicago, Illinois, part 2." Interview by Ralph H. Metcalfe,
Chicago, Illinois, May 31, 1977. Audio recording. https://www.loc.gov/item/
afc1981004_afs20667b.

Secondary Sources

Anderson, James D. *The Education of Blacks in the South, 1860–1935.* Chapel Hill: University of North Carolina Press, 1988.

Ards, Angela. "Haki Madhubuti: The Measure of a Man." *Black Issues Book Review,* March–April 2002, 43.

Baraka, Amiri. *Kawaida Studies: The New Nationalism.* Chicago: Third World Press, 1972.

"BBB Interviews Amiri Baraka." *Black Books Bulletin* 2, no. 2 (Fall 1974): 35.

"BBB Interviews Amos Wilson." *Black Books Bulletin* 7, no. 2 (1981): 36.

"BBB Interviews Barbara Sizemore." *Black Books Bulletin* 2, nos. 3 and 4 (Winter 1974): 58.

"BBB interviews Dr. Na'im Akbar." *Black Books Bulletin* 4, no. 3 (Fall 1976): 35.

"BBB Interviews Gwendolyn Brooks." *Black Books Bulletin* 2, no. 1 (1974): 34.

"BBB Interviews Hoyt Fuller." *Black Books Bulletin* 1, no. 1 (Fall 1971): 23.

"BBB Interviews Malauna Karenga." *Black Books Bulletin,* 4, no. 2 (Summer 1976): 33.

Black Allied Student Association at New York University. *Imani* 5, no. 2 (1971).

Brown, Karida L., and Charly Palmer. *The New Brownies' Book: A Love Letter to Black Families.* San Francisco: Chronicle Books, 2023.

Brown, Scot. *Fighting for US: Malauna Karenga, the US Organization, and Black Cultural Nationalism.* New York: New York University Press, 2003.

Byrd, Brandon R., Leslie M. Alexander, and Russell Rickford. *Ideas in Unexpected Places: Reimagining Black Intellectual History.* Evanston, IL: Northwestern University Press, 2022.

Clarke, Cheryl. *"After Mecca": Women Poets and the Black Arts Movement.* New Brunswick, NJ: Rutgers University Press, 2006.

Cobb, Charlie. *African Notebook: Views on Returning Home.* Chicago: Institute of Positive Education, June 1972.

Collins, Lisa Gail, and Margo Natalie Crawford, eds. *New Thoughts on the Black Arts Movement.* New Brunswick, NJ: Rutgers University Press, 2008.

Drake, St. Clair, and Horace R. Cayton. *Black Metropolis: A Study of Negro Life in a Northern City.* Chicago: University of Chicago Press, 1945.

Drum and Spear Press, *Children of Africa: A Coloring Book.* Washington, DC: Drum and Spear Press, 1972.

East, The. *Outline for a New African Educational Institution: The Uhuru Sasa Shule School Program.* Brooklyn, NY: Black Nation Education Series, 1971. Shule Jumamose Archive, Sacramento, California.

Edwards, Brent Hayes. *Epistrophies: Jazz and the Literary Imagination.* Cambridge, MA: Harvard University Press, 2017.

Farmer, Ashley D. *Remaking Black Power: How Black Women Transformed an Era.* Chapel Hill: University of North Carolina Press, 2017.

Fenderson, Jonathan. *Building the Black Arts Movement: Hoyt Fuller and the Cultural Politics of the 1960s.* Urbana: University of Illinois Press, 2019.

Fisher, Maisha T. *Black Literate Lives: Historical and Contemporary Perspectives.* New York: Routledge, 2009.

Fisher, Maisha T. "Choosing Literacy: African Diaspora Participatory Literacy Communities." PhD diss., University of California at Berkeley, 2003.

Fisher, Maisha T. "Earning Dual Degrees: Black Bookstores as Alternative Knowledge Spaces." *Anthropology and Education Quarterly* 37, no. 1 (2006): 83–99.

Fisher, Maisha T. "'Every City Has Soldiers': The Role of Intergenerational Relationships in Participatory Literacy Communities." *Research in the Teaching of English* 42, no. 2 (2007): 139–62.

Fisher, Maisha T. "The Song Is Unfinished: The New Literate and Literary and Their Institutions." *Written Communication* 21, no. 3 (2004): 290–312.

Fisher, Maisha T. *Writing in Rhythm: Spoken Word Poetry in Urban Classrooms.* New York: Teachers College Press, 2007.

Forsgren, La Donna L. *In Search of Our Warrior Mothers: Women Dramatists of the Black Arts Movement.* Evanston, IL: Northwestern University Press, 2018.

Forsgren, La Donna L. *Sistuhs in the Struggle: An Oral History of Black Arts Movement Theater and Performance.* Evanston, IL: Northwestern University Press, 2020.

Franklin, V. P. "To Be Heard in Black and White: Historical Perspectives on Black Print Culture." *Journal of African American History* 95, nos. 3 and 4 (Summer/Fall Special Issue, 2010): 291–95.

Fuller, Hoyt W. "Towards a Black Aesthetic." In *The Black Aesthetic*, edited by Addison Gayle Jr. Garden City, NY: Doubleday, 1971.

Gayle Jr., Addison, ed., *The Black Aesthetic.* Garden City, NY: Doubleday, 1971.

Gilyard, Keith. *Let's Flip the Script: An African American Discourse on Language, Literature, and Learning.* Detroit, MI: Wayne State University Press, 1996.

Givens, Jarvis R. *Fugitive Pedagogy: Carter G. Woodson and the Art of Black Teaching.* Cambridge, MA: Harvard University Press, 2021.

Giwa, Tayo, and Cynthia Gordy Giwa, writers. *The Sun Rises in the East: The Birth, Rise, and Legacy of Brooklyn's Black Nation.* Black-owned Brooklyn, 2022. 58 min.

Hayes, Worth Kamili. *Schools of Our Own: Chicago's Golden Age of Black Private Education.* Evanston, IL: Northwestern University Press, 2020.

Hilliard, Asa G., III, "I.Q. Thinking as Catechism: Ethnic and Cultural Bias or Invalid Science?" *Black Books Bulletin* 7, no. 2 (1981): 2.

Hines, Michael. *A Worthy Piece of Work: The Untold Story of Madeline Morgan and the Fight for Black History in Schools.* Boston: Beacon Press, 2022.

Holt, Thomas. "Knowledge Is Power: The Black Struggle for Literacy." In *The Right to Literacy*, edited by Andrea A. Lunsford, Helen S. Moglen, and James F. Slevin. New York: Modern Language Association of America.

Hunter, Marcus Anthony, and Zandria F. Robinson. *Chocolate Cities: The Black Map of American Life*. Oakland: University of California Press, 2018.

Iman, Kasisi Yusef. *The Weusi Alfabeti*. Brooklyn: The East, 1979.

Jarrell, Wadsworth A. *AFRICOBRA: Experimental Art Toward a School of Thought*. Durham, NC: Duke University Press, 2020.

Jemison, N. K. Introduction to *How Long 'til Black Future Month?* New York: Orbit Books, 2018.

Johansen, Bob. *Get There Early: Sending the Future to Compete in the Present*. Oakland, CA: Berrett-Koehler Publishers, 2007.

Johnson, Christine C. *ABCs of African History*. New York: Vantage Press, 1971.

Joseph, Peniel, ed. *The Black Power Movement: Rethinking the Civil Rights/Black Power Era*. London: Routledge, 2006.

Joseph, Peniel. *Waiting 'til the Midnight Hour: A Narrative History of the Black Power Movement*. New York: Macmillan Publishers, 2007.

Knupfer, Anne Meis. *The Chicago Black Renaissance and Women's Activism* Urbana: University of Illinois Press, 2006.

Konadu, Kwasi. *A View from the East: Black Cultural Nationalism and Education in New York City*. New York: Diasporic Africa Press, 2018.

Lee, Carol D. *Culture, Literacy, and Learning: Taking Bloom in the Midst of a Whirlwind*. New York: Teachers College Press, 2007.

Lee, Carol D. "Profile of an Independent Black Institution: African-Centered Education at Work." *Journal of Negro History* 61, no. 2 (1992): 161.

Lee, Carol D. "Remembering Barbara Ann Sizemore 1927–2004.*Educational Researcher* 33, no. 8 (November 2004): 37.

Lee, Don L. "What We're About." *Black Books Bulletin* 1, no. 1 (1971): 25.

Levin, Josh. *The Queen: The Forgotten Life Behind an American Myth*. New York: Back Bay Books, 2020.

Lewis, George E. *A Power Stronger than Itself: The AACM and American Experimental Music*. Chicago: University of Chicago Press, 2008.

Lillis, Theresa. "Ethnography as Method, Methodology, and 'Deep Theorizing': Closing the Gap Between Text and Context in Academic Writing and Research." *Written Communication* 25, no. 3 (2008): 353–88.

Llewellyn, Grace. *Freedom Challenge: African American Homeschoolers*. Eugene, OR: Lowry House Publishing, 1996.

Mabbott, Cass. "The We Need Diverse Books Campaign and Critical Race Theory: Charlemae Rollins and the Call for Diverse Children's Books." *Library Trends* 65, no. 4 (2017): 515–16.

Madhubuti, Haki. R. "*Black World*: The Silencing of a Giant." *Black Books Bulletin* 4, no. 2 (Summer 1976): 11.

Madhubuti, Haki R. "Foreword. Cultural Work: Planting New Trees with New Seeds." In *Too Much Schooling, Too Little Education: A Paradox of Black Life in White Societies*, ed. Mwalimu J. Shujaa. Trenton, NJ: African World Press, 1994.

Madhubuti, Haki R. *From Plan to Planet Life Studies: The Need for Afrikan Minds and Institutions*. Chicago: Third World Press, 1972, 1992.

Madhubuti, Haki R. "The Latest Purge: The Attack on Black Nationalism and Pan-Afrikanism by the New Left, the Sons and Daughters of the Old Left." *The Black Scholar* 6, no. 1 (September 1974): 43–56.

Madhubuti, Haki R., and Lasana D. Kazembe [interview], "A New Music Screaming in the Sun: Haki R. Madhubuti and the Nationalization/Internationalization of Chicago's BAM." *Chicago Review* 62, no. 4 (2019): 110.

Mahiri, Jabari. *The Day They Stole the Letter J*. Chicago: Third World Press, 1981.

Marable, Manning. *Living Black History: How Reimagining the African-American Past Can Remake America's Racial Future*. New York: Basic Civitas Books, 2006.

Markel, Seth M. "Publishers for a Pan African World: Drum and Spear Press and Tanzania's Ujamaa Ideology." *The Black Scholar* 37, no. 4 (Winter 2008): 16–26.

McDermott, Gerald. *The Magic Tree: A Tale From the Congo*. New York: Holt, Rinehart, and Winston, 1973.

McHenry, Elizabeth. *Forgotten Readers: Recovering the Lost History of African American Literary Societies*. Durham, NC: Duke University Press, 2002.

McHenry, Elizabeth, and Shirley Brice Heath. "The Literate and the Literary: African Americans as Writers and Readers 1830–1940." *Written Communication* 11, no. 4 (1994): 419–44.

Michaeli, Ethan. *The Defender: How the Legendary Black Newspaper Changed America*. Boston: Houghton Mifflin Harcourt, 2016.

Nobles, Wade. "The Black Family and Its Children: The Survival of Humaneness." *Black Books Bulletin* 6, no. 2 (1978): 8.

Nocera, Amato. "'May We Not Write Our Own Fairy Tales and Make Black Beautiful?': African American Teachers, Children's Literature, and the Construction of Race in the Curriculum, 1920–1945." *History of Education Quarterly* 63, no. 1 (2023).

Nyerere, Julius. *UJAMAA: Essays on Socialism*. Oxford: Oxford University Press, 1974.

Okoshi, Akane. *The Sun Rises in the East: A Documentary Film by Tayo Giwa and Cynthia Gordy Giwa, Discussion and Activity Guide*. Brooklyn, NY: Black-Owned Brooklyn, 2023. www.sunrisesintheeast.com.

Paris, Django, and Maisha T. Winn, eds. *Humanizing Research: Decolonizing Qualitative Research with Communities*. Thousand Oaks, CA: Sage Publishing, 2014.

Parks, Carole A. "Goodbye Black Sambo: Black Writers Forge New Images in Children's Literature." *Ebony* 28, no. 1 (November 1972): 60–62, 67–70.

Parks, Carole A. *Nommo: A Literary Legacy of Black Chicago, 1967–1987*. Chicago: Obahouse, 1987.

Penn-Nabrit, Paula. *Morning by Morning: How We Homeschooled Our African-American Sons to the Ivy League*. New York: Villard, 2003.

Perry, Imani. *Looking for Lorraine: The Radiant and Radical Life of Lorraine Hansberry*. Boston: Beacon Press, 2018.

Pinderhughes, Dianne. *Race and Ethnicity in Chicago Politics: A Reexamination of Pluralist Theory*. Urbana: University of Illinois Press, 1987.

Rickford, Russell. "Kazi Is the Blackest of All: Pan-African Nationalism and the Making of the 'New Man': 1969–1975." *Journal of African American History* 101, nos. 1–2 (Winter–Spring 2016): 99.

Rickford, Russell. *We Are An African People: Independent Education, Black Power, and the Radical Imagination*. Oxford: Oxford University Press, 2016.

Robinson, Cedric J. "Blaxploitation and the Misrepresentation of Liberation." *Race & Class* 40, no. 1 (1998): 1–12.

Robinson, Dolores. "High Blood Pressure (HYPERTENSION): The Most Serious Health Problem Faced by Blacks in America." *Black Books Bulletin* 3, no. 2 (Summer 1975): 14.

ross, kihana miraya, and Jarvis R. Givens. "The Clearing: On Black Education Studies and the Problem of Antiblackness." *Harvard Educational Review* 93, no. 2 (2023): 149–72.

Salaam, Kalamu ya. "A Response to Haki Madhubuti." *The Black Scholar* 6, no. 5 (1975): 40–53

Salaam, Kalamu ya. *The Magic of Juju: An Appreciating of the Black Arts Movement*. Chicago: Third World Press, 2016.

Salaam, Kalamu ya, and Tayari kwa Salaam. *Herufi: An Alphabet Reader*. New Orleans, LA: Kuumba Na Kazi / Ahidiana Habari, March 1978.

Salaam, Tayari kwa. "Practice the Values and Love Revolution." *Black Books Bulletin* 2, nos. 3 and 4 (Winter 1974): 49.

Salter, George. "Spinal Manipulations: A Key to Health." *Black Books Bulletin* 3, no. 2 (Summer 1975): 4–7.

Sanchez, Sonia. *It's a New Day (Poems for Young Brothas and Sistuhs)*. Detroit, MI: Broadside Press, 1971.

Sanchez, Sonia. *Wounded in the House of a Friend*. Boston: Beacon Press, 1995.

Satterwhite, Frank, ed. *Planning an Independent Black Educational Institution*. Harlem, NY: Moja Publishing House, 1971.

Shackelford, Jane D. *The Child's Story of the Negro*. Washington, DC: Associated Press, 1938.

Shujaa, Mwalimu. *Too Much Schooling, Too Little Education: A Paradox of Black Life in White Societies*. Trenton, NJ: African World Press, 1994.

Siddle Walker, Vanessa. *Hello Professor: A Black Principal and Professional Leadership in the Segregated South*. Chapel Hill: University of North Carolina Press, 2009.

Siddle Walker, Vanessa. *Their Highest Potential*. Chapel Hill: University of North Carolina Press, 1996.

Sites, William. *Sun Ra's Chicago: Afrofuturism and the City*. Chicago: University of Chicago Press, 2020.

Smethurst, James Edward. *The Black Arts Movement: Literary Nationalism in the 1960s and 1970s*. Chapel Hill: University of North Carolina Press, 2005.

Sullivan, Mary W. *Jokers Wild*. Boston: Addison-Wesley Educational Publishers, 1970.

"Tai Chi Ch'uan, the Art of Healing." *Black Books Bulletin* 3, no. 2 (Summer 1975): 36.

Todd-Breland, Elizabeth. *A Political Education: Black Politics and Education Reform in Chicago Since the 1960s*. Chapel Hill: University of North Carolina Press, 2018.

"Transcript: Library for the People Episode 2: The Library as the Soul of the Community." Library for the People podcast, June 15, 2023, https://www.chipublib.org/transcript-library-for-the-people-episode-2.

Ward, Francis. *"Super Fly": A Political and Cultural Condemnation by the Kuumba Workshop*. Chicago: Institute of Positive Education, 1972.

West, E. James. *Our Kind of Historian: The Work and Activism of Lerone Bennett Jr.* Amherst: University of Massachusetts Press, 2022.

Weusi, Kasisi Jitu. "From Relevance to Excellence: The Challenge of Independent Black Educational Institutions." *Black Books Bulletin* 2, nos. 3 and 4 (Winter 1974): 21.

Willhelm, Sidney. *Who Needs the Negro?* Cambridge, MA: Schenkman Publishing, 1970.

Williams, Jakobi. *From the Bullet to the Ballot: The Illinois Chapter of the Black Panther Party and Racial Coalition Politics in Chicago*. Chapel Hill: University of North Carolina Press, 2013.

Wilson, Amos. "The Psychological Development of the Black Child." *Black Books Bulletin* 7, no. 2 (1981): 13.

Winn, Maisha T. "Futures Matter: Creating Just Futures in This Age of Hyper-incarceration," *Peabody Journal of Education* 96, no. 5 (2021), 527–39.

Winn, Maisha T. *Girl Time: Literacy, Justice, and the School-to-Prison Pipeline*. New York: Teachers College Press, 2011.

Winn, Maisha T. *Imagining Equity: Leveraging the 5 Pedagogical Stances*. Scottsdale, AZ: Imagine Learning, 2021.

Winn, Maisha T. "Paradigm Shifting Toward Justice in Teacher Education." University of Michigan, TeachingWorks Working Paper, 2019.

Winn, Maisha T., and Joseph Ubiles. "Worthy Witnessing: Collaborative Research in Urban Classrooms." In *Studying Diversity in Teacher Education*, edited by Arnetha Ball and Cynthia Tyson. Lanham, MD: Rowman & Littlefield, 2011.

Woodard, Komozi. *A Nation Within a Nation: Amiri Baraka (LeRoi Jones) & Black Power Politics*. Chapel Hill: University of North Carolina Press, 1999.

Woodson, Carter G. *Mis-education of the Negro*. Washington, DC: Associated Publishers, 1933.

154 · FUTURING BLACK LIVES

Wright, Richard. *White Man, Listen!* Garden City, NY: Doubleday, 1957.

Zorach, Rebecca. *Art for People's Sake: Artists and Community in Black Chicago, 1965–1975.* Durham, NC: Duke University Press, 2019.

Index

Page numbers in *italic* refer to figures.

Abbot, Robert S., 121–23
ABCs of African History (children's book), 100
African Free School (Newark), 5, 7
African Street Carnival, 114
African Youth Village, 35–36
AFRICOBRA (African Commune of Bad Relevant Artists), 11, 28
Afrik, Hannibal (Harold Charles), 27, 48
Afrofuturism, 15
Ahidiana Work/Study Center (New Orleans), 23–24, 25, 36–38, 101, 115
Ahidiana-Habari, 23–24
Akbar, Na'im, 84–85
Alkalimat, Abdul (Gerald McWorter), 11
American Educational Researcher Association, 111
Amini-Hudson, Johari (née Jewell Lattimore), 81, 112–13, 130n2, 134n42, 137n3
Anderson, James, 12, 15–16
Angela Davis: Seize the Time (exhibition), 11
Arkestra, xi
Armah, Ayi Kwei, 51
Association for the Advancement of Creative Musicians, xi

Association of Black Psychologists, 85
Autobiography of Malcolm X, The (X with Haley), 59

Banneker, Benjamin, 97
Baraka, Amina, 30
Baraka, Amiri (formerly LeRoi Jones)
  Black Arts Repertory Theatre/School (BARTS) and, 10, 42, 130n7
  Black Books Bulletin (journal) and, 10, 77–78
  Black Cultural Nationalism and, 56
  fire aesthetic and, 53
  Madhubuti and, 43
  Seven Principles of Blackness (Kwanzaa) and, 77
  United Brothers and, 30
Barbara A. Sizemore Academy, 132n23, 146n15
Beat Poets, 10
Bennett, Lerone, Jr., 57–58
Bethune, Mary McCloud, 97
Betty Shabazz Academy, 132n23, 146n15
Betty Shabazz International Charter Schools (BSICS), 21–22, 113–14, 121–23, 132n23
Black Aesthetic, The (Gayle), 107-8

156 · FUTURING BLACK LIVES

Black Arts Movement
  aesthetics of, 107–8
  Black Books Bulletin (journal) and,
    72
  in Chicago, xi, 10–12, 42–43, 48
  education and, x–xii. *See also*
    Institute of Positive Education
    (IPE)
  fire aesthetic and, 53
  Independent Black Institutions
    (IBIs) and, 2–4, 25–30
  Lee and, 48
  Madhubuti and, 40, 114
  origins and history of, 10, 42
  reading and, 93–94
Black Arts Repertory Theatre/School
    (BARTS), 10, 42, 130n7
Black Books Bulletin (journal)
  Ahidiana Work/Study Center and,
    37–38
  Amini-Hudson and, 137n3
  BBB Interviews in, 72, 74–80, 75,
    83, 86
  children's literature and. *See* Books
    for the Young
  context of, 26, 66–68
  funding, production, and
    distribution of, 70–71
  health and wellness in, 81–86, 82
  inaugural issue of, 70–71, 71, 72–74,
    93, 101–2, 118
  IPE Baraza ya Kazi image in, 1–3, 2,
    64, 112, 118
  Lee and, 40–41
  Madhubuti and, 10, 40, 63, 67, 70–
    74, 90–91, 92–93, 118
  Mahiri and, 2, 41, 59–60, 68–69, 75–
    76, 90, 99, 109–10
  mission and importance of, x–xi,
    2, 10–11, 12, 55–56, 62, 63–66,
    70–74

  Moyo and, 68, 81–82
  Olu and, 63–64, 65, 91–92
  Pan-Africanism and, 3, 66, 96–97
  Third World Press and, 68–70
  Walton and, 55
Black Boy (Wright), 43–44
Black Collegian, The (magazine), 68, 80
Black Cultural Nationalism
  Black Books Bulletin (journal) and, 3,
    64–66, 78–79
  Congress of African People and,
    30–31
  Institute of Positive Education and,
    22, 56
  Karenga and, 56, 64–65
  See also Congress of African People
Black education
  Black Arts Movement and, x–xii
  Black Books Bulletin (journal) and,
    85–86
  Black print culture and, 25–38
  Black psychology and, 85–86
  Identity, Purpose, and Direction as
    pillars of, xi–xii, 3, 5, 25, 88, 105
  See also children's literature;
    Institute of Positive Education
    (IPE)
Black Education Studies, 16
Black Experience in Sound, 35–36
Black Fire (Jones and Neal), 53
Black News (newspaper), 26, 34, 35–
  36, 68, 115
Black newspapers, 10, 22–23, 26,
  67–68
Black Pages (pamphlet series), 2, 40,
  92, 98
Black Panther Party, 77, 114
Black Panther, The (newspaper), 26
Black Position, The (magazine), 80
Black Power Movement, 2–3, 25–30,
  93–94

Black print culture
  BBB Interviews and, 80
  in Chicago, 22–23, 42
  children's literature and, ix–x, 89–
    90, 95
  Fuller and, 11, 42, 67, 79–80, 129n1
  as literary activism, 66–68
  See also Black newspapers
Black psychology, 84–86
Black Rituals (Plumpp), 70
Black Scholar, The (journal), 46, 67, 80
Black self-determination
  Black Books Bulletin (journal) and,
    66, 94, 96
  Congress of African People and, 31
  The East and, 35
  futuring and, x, 9–10, 13–14
  Institute of Positive Education and, 64
Black World (formerly *Negro Digest*)
  (magazine), 11, 42, 67, 79–80,
  129n1
Black-Owned Brooklyn, 114–15
Blackstone Rangers, 11
Blaxploitation films, 91–93
Bontemps, Arna, ix–x
Books for the Young
  on beauty and purpose, 106–8, 109–
    10
  on *Children of Africa* (coloring book),
    94–97
  context and mission of, 72, 89–94
  on harmful stereotypes, 101–6
  on *The Magic Tree* (McDermott),
    87–89
  Mahiri and, 90, 99, 109–10, 112
  nation building and, 89, 94–101, 110
Breaking the Chains of Psychological
  Slavery (Akbar), 84
Broadside Press, 46–47, 67, 72, 110
Brooks, Gwendolyn, ix–x, 11, 69–70,
  80, 108–9, 117–18

Brown, Oscar, Jr., 11
Brownies' Book, The (magazine), 105
Burroughs, Charles, 10, 42, 46
Burroughs, Margaret, ix–x

California Association for Afro
  American Education, 30–31
Campbell, Les. *See* Weusi, Jitu
"Catch the Fire" (Sanchez), 53
Catholic Church, 21–22
Cayton, Horace R., 22
Charles, Harold (Hannibal Afrik), 27,
  48
Charles, Ray, 97–98
Chicago
  Black Arts Movement in, xi, 10–12,
    42–43, 48
  Black print culture in, 22–23, 42
  Independent Black Institutions
    (IBIs) in, 25–30. *See also* Institute
    of Positive Education (IPE)
  Red Summer Riots (1919) in, 49
Chicago Defender, The (newspaper),
  22–23
Chicago Teachers Union, 48
Children of Africa (coloring book),
  94–98
children's literature
  beauty and purpose in, 106–10
  Black Books Bulletin (journal) and.
    See Books for the Young
  Black print culture and, ix–x, 89–90,
    95
  nation building and, 89, 94–101, 110
  Third World Press and, 90, 95, 98–
    101, 108–9, 112
Child's Story of the Negro, The
  (Shackelford), 105–6
Childtimes (Greenfield), 107
Chrisman, Robert, 67
citizen archivists, 25

158 · FUTURING BLACK LIVES

Clifton, Lucille, 107
Cobb, Charlie, 98
collective work
  in Books for the Young reviews, 97, 104
  futuring as, 9–10, 16
  at Institute of Positive Education (IPE), 42, 47, 61–62, 73–74, 89, 113–19
Committee for a Unified Newark, 30–32, 68
Community of Self, The (Akbar), 84
Communiversity, 11
Congress of African People, 77–78, 81, 114. *See also* East, The (Brooklyn); *Planning an Independent Black Educational Institution* (Congress of African People)
Conservator, The (newspaper), 22
Coogler, Ryan, 114
Cooperative Economics (Ujamaa), 24, 36, 116
Council of Independent Black Institutions, 114, 132n23
COVID-19 pandemic, 4–5
Cricket, The (journal), 43
cultural modeling, 48–49

Daley, Richard J., 26
Datcher, Michael, 60
Davis, Angela, 11
Day They Stole Letter J, The (Mahiri), 110, 112
Dent, Tom, 67–68
Destruction of Black Civilization, The (Williams), 68
Dill, Augustus Granville, 105
distributed leadership, 61–62. *See also* collective work
Donaldson, Jeff, 28
Dr. Seuss, 142n4

Drake, St. Claire, 22
Drum and Spear, 72, 94–98
Du Bois, W. E. B., 74–75, 105
Dumas, Alexander, 44
DuSable Black History Museum and Education Center (formerly Ebony Museum of Negro History and Art) (Chicago), 10, 42, 46, 83

East, The (Brooklyn), 5, 7, 17, 101, 114–15. *See also* Black News (newspaper); *Outline for a New African Educational Institution* (The East)
East Records, 35–36
Ebony (magazine), ix, 49, 58, 67, 79–80, 90
Ebony Jr. (magazine), 90
Ebony Museum of Negro History and Art (now DuSable Black History Museum and Education Center) (Chicago), 10, 42, 46, 83
education. *See* Black education
Edwards, Brent Hayes, 42–43
Essence (magazine), 80
Evans, Mari, 70

Farmer, Ashley, 30
Farrakhan, Louis, 67
Fauset, Jessie Redmon, 105
Fenderson, Jonathan, 79–80
Ferdinand, Val (later Kalamu ya Salaam), 67–68
Field Enterprises, 103
Fields-Smith, Cheryl, 131n10
Final Call, The (newspaper), 67
fire, 53
Fisher, Cheryl Ann (formerly Cheryl Ann Smith), 5–8
Fisher, James Adolphus, 6–8, 11, 34, 131n15

Floyd, George, 4–5
forecasting, 9–10, 40, 43. *See also* futuring
foresight, 13–14, 78–79, 113
Fritz, Angela, 133n35
Frog and Toad Are Friends (Lobel), 142n4
From Plan to Planet Life Studies (Madhubuti), 5, 30, 67
fugitive pedagogy, 16
Fuller, Hoyt W., 11, 42, 67, 79–80, 129n1
Fulton, Alvenia, 83
Future Shock (Toffler), 47–48
future-oriented historiography, 15
futuring
    as collective work, 9–10, 16, 23
    concept of, x–xi, 9–10, 23
    forecasting and, 9–10, 40, 43
    Historiography for the Future and, 13–17, 113–19

Garvey, Marcus Mosiah, 56, 74–75, 94
Gayle, Addison, Jr., 107–8
gentrification, 114–15
"Gettin' it Together: A Service Conference on Black Survival" (1971), 5–6, 6
Givens, Jarvis, 16
Giwa, Cynthia Gordy, 114–15
Giwa, Tayo, 114–15
Goncalves, Joe, 67
"Goodbye Black Sambo" (Parks), ix
Gorman, Bertha, 5–6
Greenfield, Eloise, 97, 107
Gregory, Dick, 74, 83
Gwendolyn Brooks Writers House, 121–23

Hamilton, Virginia, ix
Hampton, Fred, 58
Hansberry, Lorraine, 104

happy slave tropes, 105
Hardman, Della, 137–38n4
Hare, Nathan, 67
Harsh, Vivian, ix–x
Hayes, Worth Kamili, 17, 43, 114
health and wellness, 81–86, 82
Henry Holt & Company, 87–89
Herufi (children's book), 101
Hieroglyphics Ink, 70–71
Hilliard, Asa, 84, 85–86
historical ethnography, 13
historical signals, 16
Historiography for the Future, 13–17, 113–19
homeschooling, 4–5
Hughes, Langston, ix–x
Hunter, Marcus Anthony, 27
Hurston, Zora Neale, ix–x

I Want To Be (children's book), 98–101
Identity, Purpose, and Direction, xi–xii, 3, 5, 25, 88, 105
Iman, Kasisi Yusef, 101
Imani (magazine), 130n3
In the Night Kitchen (Sendak), 142n4
Independent Black Institutions (IBIs), 2–4, 25–30. *See also* Institute of Positive Education (IPE)
Institute for the Future, 4
Institute of Positive Education (IPE)
    Baraza ya Kazi (work council) of, 1–3, 2, 64, 112, 118
    co-founders and visionaries at, 39–43, 61–62. *See also specific visionaries*
    collective work at, 42, 47, 61–62, 73–74, 89, 113–19
    context of, 25–30, 42–43
    history of, 11–13, 21–23, 39–40
    legacy and values of, x–xii, 5, 7, 113–14, 115–19

Institute of Positive Education
(*continued*)
See also *Black Books Bulletin*
(journal); New Concept
Development Center
International African Arts Festival, 114
IQ testing, 85–86
"It's Nation Time" (Baraka), 10

Jackie (Jolly), 108
Jackson, John Shenoy, xi
Jemison, N. K., 13
Jet (magazine), 49, 67, 80
Jihad Productions, 72
Johnson Publishing Company, 11, 42,
67, 79–80, 90
Jokers Wild (Sullivan), 102–3
Jolly, Cheryl, 108
Jones, LeRoi. *See* Baraka, Amiri
Jordan, June, ix
Journal of Black Poetry (journal), 67, 80
Julien, Mtumishi St., 36. See also
Operating Principles (St. Julien)

Karenga, Malauna
Black Books Bulletin (journal) and,
63–65, 78–79, 80
Black Cultural Nationalism and, 56,
64–65
Institute of Positive Education and,
121–22
Madhubuti and, 138n11
See also Seven Principles of
Blackness (Kwanzaa)
Kawaida Studies (Baraka), 77
kazi (work), 81–82
Kelley, Robin D. G., 15

Know Thy Self (Akbar), 84
Kununuana (food co-op), 35–36
Kuumba Theatre Workshop, 11, 58, 92
Kwanzaa. *See* Seven Principles of
Blackness

Lattimore, Jewell. *See* Amini-Hudson,
Johari (née Jewell Lattimore)
Lawson, Jennifer, 98
Lee, Carol D. (née Easton) (Safisha
Madhubuti)
on Amini-Hudson, 134n42
IPE Baraza ya Kazi and, 1–3, *2*, 64,
112, 118
as IPE visionary, x–xi, 21, 25–26, 27,
40–41, 48–52, 59, 61–62, 111–14,
115–17
life and career of, 48–52, 70
New Concept Development Center
and, 47, 48
photographs of, 1–3, *2*, 52, *55*, 64,
112, 118
Lee, Don L. *See* Madhubuti, Haki R.
Lee, Helen Maxine Graves, 43–44
Lewis, Norman, 106
Liberator (magazine), 80
Lillis, Theresa, 145n2
Listen for the Fig Tree (Mathis), 104–5
Lobel, Arnold, 142n4
local/national/local (L/N/L) model, 24
Lorax, The (Dr. Seuss), 142n4

Madhubuti, Haki R. (formerly Don L.
Lee)
on Anderson, 12
on art, 42–43, 44–45, 59
on Black Arts Movement, 11

Black Books Bulletin (journal) and,
  10, 40, 63, 67, 70–74, 90–91, 92–
  93, 118
Brooks and, 70
Fuller and, 11, 79, 80
IPE Baraza ya Kazi and, 1–3, *2*, 64,
  112, 118
as IPE visionary, x–xi, 21–22, 28, 29,
  39–40, 41–42, 43–48, 59, 61–62,
  112–14, 117, 119, 123
Kuumba Theatre Workshop and, 92
Lee and, 48, 50
life and career of, 43–48
Mahiri and, 39–40, 59–60
Moyo and, 58
Organization of Black American
  Culture and, 11
photographs of, 1–3, *2*, *52*, 64, 112, 118
telecommuting and, 13
Third World Press and, 1–2, 40, 108
Walton and, 52–53
Magic Tree, The (McDermott), 87–89
Mahiri, Jabari (formerly Cleve
  Washington)
Black Books Bulletin (journal) and, 2,
  41, 59–60, 68–69, 75–76, 90, 99,
  109–10
on Brooks, 117–18
children's literature and, 90, 99, 109–
  10, 112
IPE Baraza ya Kazi and, 1–3, *2*, 64,
  112, 118
as IPE visionary, 39–40, 41, 59–61,
  111–14
life and career of, 39–40, 59–61, 70
photographs of, 1–3, *2*, *52*, *55*, 64,
  112, 118

Man Who Cried I Am, The (Williams),
  59
Marxism, 46, 77, 114
Mason, Baba Shannon Sundiata, 121–23
Mathis, Sharon Bell, ix, 103–4
McDermott, Gerald, 87–89
McWorter, Gerald (Abdul Alkalimat),
  11
Michaeli, Ethan, 22–23
Mis-Education of the Negro (Woodson),
  31–32, 34
Moyo, K. Kofi, *2*, 64, 130n1
Moyo, Kimya (née Saundra Malone)
  Black Books Bulletin (journal) and,
    68, 81–82
  as IPE visionary, 28, 29, 41, 51–52,
    56–59, 61–62, 112–13, 117, 119,
    123
  life and career of, 56–59
Muhammad Speaks (newspaper), 67

nation building, x, 89, 94–101, 110
Nation of Islam, 60–61, 67
Nation Studies, 2, 68–70
National Council of Teachers of
  English, x
Neal, Larry, 53
"Need for Afrikan education, The"
  (Madhubuti), 47
Negro Digest (later *Black World*)
  (magazine), 11, 42, 67, 79–80,
  129n1
New Concept Development Center
  (now New Concept School)
children of IPE founders at, 61–62
history of, 2, 21, 85, 121–23, 146n15
as IPE visionary, 41

New Concept Development Center
(*continued*)
Lee and, 47, 48
Moyo and, 58–59
Walton and, 54–55
New York Times (newspaper), 104
Nguzo Saba. *See* Seven Principles of
Blackness (Kwanzaa)
NKOMBO (journal), 38, 67–68
Nobles, Wade, 84, 121–22
Nommo (Parks), 129n1
Northwestern University, 56–58
Nyerere, Mwalimu Julius, 29

Oak Park School of Afro-American
Thought, 7, 8
Olu, Yaoundé, 63–64, 65, 91–92,
133n34
Operating Principles (St. Julien), 23–
24, 25, 36–38, 115
Operation Breadbasket (later
Operation PUSH), 27, 48
oral history, 42–43
Organization of Black American
Culture, 11, 42, 129n1
*Outline for a New African Educational
Institution* (The East), 23–24, 25,
33–36, 37

Pan-Africanism
Black Books Bulletin (journal) and, 3,
66, 96–97
Institute of Positive Education and,
22, 56, 116–17, 122
Parks, Carole A., ix, x
Parks, Rosa, 97

participatory literacy communities, 26
Perry, Imani, 10
Pinkney, Jerry, 107
*Planning an Independent Black
Educational Institution* (Congress
of African People), 23–24, 25,
30–33, 34
Plumpp, Sterling, 70, 137n3
Portelli, Alessandro, 42–43
Pushkin, Alexander, 44

Ra, Sun, xi
Randall, Dudley, 46–47, 67
reading, 93–94. *See also* children's
literature
Red Summer Riots (1919), 49
Reed, Ishmael, 121–22
Reid, Martha, 5–6
retrofuturism, 15, 133n34
Review of Black Political Economy
(journal), 80
Rickford, Russell, 77, 138–39n14
Rivers, Conrad Kent, 11
Robinson, Dolores, 83–84
Robinson, Zandria F., 27
Rodgers, Carolyn, 130n2
Rollins, Charlemae Hill, ix–x
Rosa Parks (Greenfield), 97
ross, kihana m., 16
Rouault, Georges, 106

Sacramento City College (SCC), 7
Salaam, Kalamu ya (né Val
Ferdinand), 24, 36, 67–68
Salaam, Tayari kwa, 37, 115–17
Sanchez, Sonia, 53, 70, 110

Satterwhite, Frank, 32
Self-Determination (Kujichagulia), 24.
    See also Black self-determination
Sendak, Maurice, 142n4
Seven Principles of Blackness
    (Kwanzaa)
  Ahidiana Work/Study Center and, 37
  Black Books Bulletin (journal) and, 77
  Black print culture and, 24
  children's literature and, 100–101
  Congress of African People and, 30
  The East and, 35, 116
  Institute of Positive Education and,
    42, 47, 114
  See also specific principles
Shabazz, Betty, 146n15
Shackelford, Jane Dabney, 105–6
Shujaa, Mwalimu, 12, 15–16
Shule Jumamose (Saturday School),
    5–9, 15, 24–25, 34, 113
Shule ya Watoto, 27, 48
Sizemore, Barbara, 74, *75*, 76–77, 78,
    146n15
Smethurst, James, 24, 138n6
Society of Umbra, 67
Soulbook (journal), 67, 80
South Side Community Art Center, 10
Steptoe, John, ix, 106–7
Stevie (Steptoe), 106–7
Sullivan, Mary W., 102–3

TAMU-Swee-Teast (restaurant), 35–36
Tanzania Publishing House, 98
Tarry, Ellen, ix
Taylor-Burroughs, Margaret, 10, 42, 46
Teacup Full of Roses (Mathis), 103–5

telecommuting, 13
"They Demanded Courageously: The
    1968 Bursar's Office Take Over"
    (exhibition), 139n26
Third World Press
  Amini and, 137n3
  Black Books Bulletin (journal) and,
    68–70
  Brooks and, 70, 108–9
  children's literature and, 90, *95*, 98–
    101, 108–9, 112
  history of, 11–12, 21–23, 26, 121–23
  Lee and, 40–41
  Madhubuti and, 1–2, 40, 108
  Moyo and, 41
  Plumpp and, 70
  Seven Principles of Blackness
    (Kwanzaa) and, 77
Tiger Who Wore White Gloves, The
    (Brooks), 108–9
Till, Emmett, 49
Till-Mobley, Mamie Elizabeth, 49
Todd-Breland, Elizabeth, 17, 53–54
Toffler, Alvin, 13, 47–48
Two Thousand Seasons (Armah), 51

Ubiles, Joseph, 138n8
Uhuru Sasa Shule (Freedom Now
    School), 17, 33–36, 101, 114
Ujamaa (Cooperative Economics), 24,
    36, 116
Ujamaa Food Co-op, 2
Ujima (Collective Work &
    Responsibility), 24, 42, 47, 89,
    104. *See also* collective work
Umbra (journal), 67

Umoja (Unity), 36, 47
United Brothers, 30
United Negro Improvement
 Association, 94
Unity & Struggle (newspaper), 26, 68

Vegetarianism (Fulton), 83

Walker, Margaret, 44
Walker, Vanessa Siddle, 15–16, 131n15
Wall of Respect, 11
Walton, Soyini (née Rochelle Ricks)
 as IPE visionary, 3, 12, 22, 23, 41,
  48, 51–56, 59, 61–62, 112–13, 118
 life and career of, 52–56
 Moyo and, 82
 photographs of, 55
Ward, Val Gray, 58
Washington, Booker T., 74–75
Washington, Cleve. *See* Mahiri, Jabari
We Build Together (Rollins), x
welfare queen trope, 103

Welsing, Francis Cress, 84
Weusi, Jitu (formerly Les Campbell),
 17, 34, 53, 66
Weusi Alfabeti, The (Iman), 101
Wheatley, Phillis, 44
White Man, Listen! (Wright), 44
Who Needs the Negro? (Willhelm),
 129–30n5
Wilcox, Preston, 32–33, 35
Willhelm, Sidney, 129–30n5
Williams, Chancellor, 68
Williams, Eugene, 49
Williams, Jakobi, 49
Williams, John A., 59
Wilson, Amos, 84, 86
women, 30, 42, 61
Woodson, Carter G., 31–32, 34
Wright, Richard, ix–x, 43–45

X, Malcolm, 10, 34, 42, 59, 130n7

Yellow Black (Madhubuti), 45